ENDORSEMENTS

"I have appreciated my friendship with I ⬛⬛⬛⬛⬛⬛⬛⬛⬛⬛⬛⬛⬛⬛⬛⬛⬛⬛⬛ is unashamed of his love for Jesus. He has been an outspoken and consistent testimony of the gospel through times of glory and trials. I love that about him."

Francis Chan, PASTOR & SPEAKER
AUTHOR, *Crazy Love: Overwhelmed by a Relentless God and Erasing Hell*

"David Akers and I were teammates for most of my thirteen years as a safety with the Philadelphia Eagles. And when it comes to his faith in God, David is the real deal. His faith increased over the years as he came to understand that God's love is bigger than our feelings. That His love, coupled with our faith, is limitless! No matter what is put in our paths! David lived out his faith on the field, in the locker room, and in every other part of his life. When David says something, it speaks volumes because his life backs it up."

Brian Dawkins, NINE-TIME PRO-BOWL SAFETY
Philadelphia Eagles and Denver Broncos

"David Akers is an unusual human being. I heard about his Christian testimony before I became Chaplain of the Philadelphia Eagles several years ago. All that I heard about him—as impressive as it was—did not begin to explain his commitment to Kingdom work. David exceeded all of my expectations. He never missed a chapel service. He never missed an opportunity to share his faith in the presence of hundreds or in the presence of one individual. I was able to witness the power of his testimony, firsthand. It made a difference, not only in the lives of players on the Philadelphia Eagles football team, but also the Eagles' administration. I was honored not only to serve him as Chaplain of the Philadelphia Eagles, but more important to me, to be called his friend.

His book will not only be a blessing to football fans, it will be a blessing to all."

Rev., Dr. H.H. Lusk II, PASTOR, GREATER EXODUS BAPTIST CHURCH, PHILADELPHIA, PA
FOUNDER AND CEO, *People for People, Inc. and Stand for Africa*
TEAM CHAPLAIN, *Philadelphia Eagles*

"I've known David for years now, and his passion for the Lord is a huge encouragement to me. He doesn't do things half-hearted, and I love the way he keeps going deeper in his faith and allows God to keep shining through him."

Jeremy Camp, SOLO ARTIST AND SONGWRITER
Five-Time Dove Award Winner & Grammy Nominee

"I had the privilege of being David's team Chaplain for one season in Detroit. From the first day he walked in our locker room, he made an impact for the kingdom of God. He walks the talk and exudes a firm and contagious faith in Jesus. I have seen many players come and go in my thirty years as Chaplain, and I can honestly say that David is as solid a Christian and evangelist as any I've mentored. [His teammates] like him—a lot—and that's not always easy for a kicker to accomplish…. His impact outside the locker room was very strong as well. He earned great respect in the community and has a love for people that is easily seen. He cares about the poorest of the poor. He preaches with power and is grounded in God's Word. I am a better man for having David in Detroit for the short time he played for the Lions."

David Wilson, LEAD PASTOR, KENSINGTON CHURCH, KENSINGTON, MI
Team Chaplain, Detroit Lions

"Yes, David Akers can kick a football. He's one of the best in history, actually. But there's more to David than you'll ever see on any given Sunday. He's been a pillar in his community, an elder in his church, an involved father, and a loyal friend. He's been through his share of highs and lows, which as a sports hero, gives him the unique ability to relate to just about anybody. And he's never too proud to talk about his challenges in life; in fact he's pretty good at it. David has taken some of the most taxing times in his life in stride—and used them as positives. And we're not just talking about a few lost games here and there. David has overcome all kinds of adversities, and he has emerged as a true hero. David's a Kentucky boy who's come a long way, and he has plenty of amazing stories to tell from his journey."

Brandon Heath, SOLO ARTIST AND SONGWRITER
Five-Time Dove Award Winner & Grammy Nominee

"David has been trusted by God to have a position in life that very few people will ever have. But what sets David apart from most professional athletes is that, instead of using those things for himself, he's leveraged it to benefit others—many of whom could never pay him back. This book will not only encourage your faith but will hopefully spur you on toward love and good deeds!"

Christian Huang, EXECUTIVE DIRECTOR
San Francisco City Impact

WINNING
IN SPITE OF

How to Turn Hard Times Into Personal Growth, Renewed Purpose, and Increased Influence

DAVID AKERS

<small>WITH</small> Mark Vermillion

REDEMPTION
PRESS

FIRST EDITION, 2015

Printed in the United States of America
by **Redemption Press, PO Box 427, Enumclaw, WA 98022**
www.redemption-press.com

www.davidakersministries.com

Discounts available for bulk orders of 10 or more copies.

For orders, speaker information, or other inquiries about the book, go to *greenakerspromotions.com.*

ISBN: 978-1-68314-105-1 Print
       978-1-68314-106-8 ePub
       978-1-68314-107-5 Mobi
Library of Congress Catalog Card Number: 2016945815

To all of my football teammates who over the years have contributed to my success as a player. And to all of my life teammates who've contributed to my development as a husband, father, friend, businessman, and Christ-follower.

I owe you a debt of gratitude.

----

*To my children, Luke, Halley, and Sawyer.
I thank God each and every day for the oportunity
to be your dad. You have blessed me
beyond measure, and I am proud that Jesus
is in the center of your lives.*

*And to my closest teammate of all, my wife, Erika.
Your name is on many of the pages in this book because
you have contributed most to every aspect of my life.*

I owe you the greatest debt of gratitude.

CONTENTS

Winning Redefined

[What I've Learned About Winning and Losing]

"*You were born to be a player. You were meant to be here. This moment is yours.*"

– HERB BROOKS –

"*You and I are the players, God's our head coach, and we're all playing the biggest game of all.*"

– JOE GIBBS –

God blessed me with a long and eventful NFL career. In fifteen years as a placekicker, I had the opportunity to play with some great teams, for some terrific coaches, and in some big games.

I played my first twelve seasons (1999-2010) for Andy Reid and the Philadelphia Eagles, the next two seasons (2011-12) for Jim Harbaugh and the San Francisco 49ers, and my final year (2013) for Jim Schwartz and the Detroit Lions. In those fifteen seasons, my teams made the playoffs ten times and reached the NFC Championship game seven times.

And I played twice in the NFL's pinnacle game—the Super Bowl.

My first Super Bowl appearance was in my fifth season (2004), when I played for the Eagles. We lost the game to the New England Patriots, 24-21. We jumped out into a lead in the first half but couldn't hold on to it in the second. It was one of those rare Super Bowl games that was competitive and exciting. Even though my team lost, I'll never forget my first super-hyped Super Bowl experience.

My second time in the Super Bowl was near the end of my career in 2012, when I played for the 49ers. My team lost that one, too—a 34-31 heartbreaker to John Harbaugh's Baltimore Ravens.
The Ravens jumped out to a 28-6 lead on us by halftime. I scored our only points in the first half.

And then the lights went out. Literally.

With 13:22 left in the third quarter, the power went out around the New Orleans Superdome, and the players stood around in the dark for thirty-four minutes until the power and lights came back on. I think all of us—players, coaches, NFL officials, city officials, the electric company, the media, and fans—were in a state of shock.

If you were watching, you probably couldn't believe it either. Once the novelty of the blackout wore off, it didn't make for very good television. But it turned out to be a blessing in disguise for my 49ers, because it changed the momentum of the game.

We came back and had a chance to win it at the end. We were down by five with less than a minute to go, and we had the ball inside our five yard line. Sadly, we couldn't punch it into the end zone in three tries, and we turned the ball over on fourth down.

And that was it. The Ravens then took an intentional safety and left us with no more time to score.

Although I made all of my kicks in that Super Bowl, it was a hard loss for everyone on our team—not to mention our fans.

Few other kickers have had the chance to play in so many big post-season games, and I'm really thankful for those opportunities to experience professional sports at its highest level.

In addition to team accomplishments, I also had some personal bright spots interspersed throughout my career. Six times I was selected to play in the Pro Bowl, the NFL all-star game, which used to be played in Hawaii the week after the Super Bowl. Only one other kicker has played in more Pro Bowls.

In 2012, I tied the record for the longest field goal in NFL history when I kicked a sixty-three yarder at Lambeau Field in Green Bay. It was a line-drive kick that thumped off the bottom cross bar and bounced through the uprights. Of course, I called the bank shot so it still counted! (In case you missed it, that was a joke. A bad one, right?)

At that time, I shared the record with Tom Dempsey (New Orleans), Jason Elam (Denver), and Sebastian Janikowski (Oakland). For a short time, that feat even got my name in the Guinness Book of World Records. My kids loved that!

But as they say, records are made to be broken. Just fourteen months later (in December 2013), Matt Prater broke the field goal distance record by kicking a sixty-four yarder in Denver.

But c'mon. He kicked it in Denver!

So, I jokingly put my own asterisk next to Prater's kick. Dempsey and I are still the only ones who've made our record kicks outside of Denver—without the mile-high altitude and rarified air that allows the ball to travel farther. I figure that's something, right?

In 2010, the NFL named me to its All-Decade Team for the 2000s (the years 2000-2009). Colts' kicker Adam Vinatieri was named as the AFC kicker of the decade, and I was named as the NFC kicker of the decade. It was an incredible honor to be on the All-Decade Team with the likes of Peyton Manning, Tom Brady, Ray Lewis, and others who are considered among the greatest players of all time. Many of those players are still my good friends.

As you can see, I've had a lot to be thankful for in my time with the NFL.

The Rest of the Story

But my NFL story doesn't stop at personal accolades and championship games. For every high point in my career, it seemed like there was a low point to offset it. Like everybody else, I've had periods of suffering, seasons of pain, and times of professional failure—on and off the field.

Off the field, my family and I have gone through financial loss, health issues, miscarriages, and struggles with depression. (You'll read more about these in the chapters ahead.)

And on the field, I missed some big kicks. Although I made four hundred and seventy-seven kicks in my career, I also missed ninety-one.

And a few of them were really big misses!

But the hardship and failure went beyond missed kicks. At the beginning of my career, I got a shot to play for three different NFL teams, and I was released by all of them before I finally made it with the Philadelphia Eagles. I nearly gave up before my career began!

And even though I played in lots of big games throughout my career, I was on the losing side of most of them. The teams I played for lost in both Super Bowls; lost in five of my seven NFC championship games; and lost in five of the seven Pro Bowls.

Translation: My big-game winning percentage is not very good.

Late in my career, at age thirty-eight, and after coming off the worst statistical year of my career, I had to search for a new team. At the time, I thought my career was over.

Like every other person I know, my life and career have had both good and bad times. Some of the good times were really good. And some of the bad times were really bad. And you know what? Looking back, I'm thankful to God for both the good and the bad.

Looking Back

In 2014, I officially retired from the NFL, and since then, I've had more time to reflect on my career. This book is the result. It contains lots of stories from my NFL experiences. But it's about much more than that. It focuses more on what I've learned along the way—about life, about God, about family, about work, about purpose, and ultimately, about what it means to be a winner.

My career as an NFL placekicker is central to the book—and my stories will give you a glimpse of what it's like to be a professional football player. But the principles in it are more about life itself. These principles come straight from God's Word, so they apply to every part of life.

And they don't just apply to me; they apply to your life, too. Your work. Your family. Your relationship with God. And your sense of purpose.

We're all human, and we've all experienced good times and bad. We all know what it's like to succeed, and we all know what it's like to fail. In the NFL, our failures are seen on national TV in front of millions of people. You've probably not failed in front of that many people, but I'm guessing you've fallen flat on your face in front of others a time or two.

Your circumstances are different than mine. And you've experienced pain I'll never fully understand. I don't know about you, but I sometimes compare my circumstances to others. That's a dumb thing to do. There will always be others who have it easier than us, and there will always be others who have it worse.

In reality, your suffering is hard for you, and my suffering is hard for me. It doesn't matter whose suffering is worse. It's just plain hard.

As I look back over my life and career, I can see God's active involvement in both my successes and failures. But at the time, I didn't always see His involvement in my failures. Sometimes it seemed like he had abandoned me. I'm sure you've never felt that way, right?

But time has a way of putting life into perspective. In hindsight, I now see that God really was involved in even the smallest details of my life. I've gotten a glimpse of why things might have happened the way they did. I'm now more fully aware of how God was involved in each part of my career.

Each season. Each game. Each kick.

In the pages ahead, I'll share with you some examples of how God has worked in my life through pain and hardship, and how He helped me to win in spite of them. It shows that hard times have been important to my life because they've brought me closer to God, and they've helped push me deeper into His Word for understanding.

God has made me a very different person than I was when I started my NFL journey in the late nineties. And the Bible has changed the way I look at everything in life.

Winning By the Book

As a professional athlete, I've continuously worked with people who are obsessed with winning. Winning is the goal of every game, and winning a championship is the goal of every season.

My performances were judged by whether or not I helped my team win games and championships.

It's pretty easy to define winning when it comes to sports. If you have more points than your opponent at the end of the game, you win. If you win enough of the time, people call you a winner.

But it's not so easy to define winning when it comes to life. That's why I want to take a "time out" early in this book to explain what I mean when I write about winning. It's a perspective that's been shaped and reshaped by God's Word.

Biblical winning is different than the world's view of winning. And winning in life is much more important than winning in sports. The stakes are higher.

After reading through the Bible, and after reflecting back over my experiences of winning and losing (on the field and off), I would define winning in life this way:

Win-ning, v. 1. *Overcoming the hardships and obstacles in life to emerge victorious in the areas that are important to God;*
2. *Staying faithful and obedient to God and His Word, regardless of how hard it is;*
3. *Hearing God say, "Well done."*

Here's the thing. We can't win all the time in every area of life. So, we have to focus our priorities on the things that are most important to God, and give our greatest efforts in those areas. But often, the things that are important to God aren't the things that are important to the world—or to us.

Here's an example: We know that one of the most important things to God is people. The most famous verse in the Bible, John 3:16, says that God loves people and gave His Son to suffer and die for them. So, if you're stepping on people to get where you want to go, you may be a winner in the eyes of others, but you'll never be a winner in the eyes of God.

Ultimately, God defines winning. Not by you and me.

Pressing On

Church historians believe that the apostle Paul was an athlete. He was definitely familiar with the games during his time. He used a bunch of sports metaphors when writing his letters to different

New Testament churches.

Here's my favorite of Paul's sports metaphors:

"I press on take hold of that for which Christ Jesus took hold of me. Brothers, I do not consider myself yet to have taken hold of it. But one thing I do: Forgetting what is behind and straining toward what is ahead, I press on toward the goal to win the prize for which God has called me heavenward in Christ Jesus" (Philippians 3:12b-14).

Do you hear the sense of passion and purpose in Paul's words? He used words like straining and pressing on. This should be a clue that winning is hard. It means that to win, we'll have to overcome obstacles and persevere.

The word *straining* reminds me of the P90X workouts I've done throughout the off-seasons of my career. They are hardcore. I was so into P90X at one time that I became a paid endorser for them.

One of the things I like about the program is that it provides a different workout each day. The workouts are designed to create "muscle confusion," which keeps you from ever plateauing in your workout.

I also like P90X because the results of my workouts are really up to me. I'll get as much out of it as I put into it. The more I strain, the closer I'll get to my reward. So I strain toward what is ahead and press on toward my goals.

Whenever you do any kind of strength training, the key is to press hard enough to strain your muscles so that you actually cause them to tear. Sounds counter-intuitive, doesn't it? Tearing your muscles sounds like a bad thing, but when you strain your muscles in a controlled workout, you actually cause micro-tears in the tissue that then heal and cause the muscle to grow bigger and stronger.

So, straining your muscles is really a good thing that makes you able to handle more in the future. The same thing happens when we strain and press on with our spiritual lives.

As they say "No pain, no gain."

Paul was willing to go through the pain to get to the gain. For him, the prize at the end of his lifelong race was Heaven. That's why he was willing to work so hard. That's why he hung in there and pressed on.

The prize was so worth it.

It's worth it for you and me, as well. That's why I've written this book.

It's hard to hang in there when times get really hard, and it feels like everything in your world is falling apart. I want to help you not give up. I want to help you persevere so that you, too, will win the prize—in spite of your suffering and failures.

Winning the Prize

Here's another favorite sports metaphors from Paul:

"Do you not know that in a race all the runners run, but only one gets the prize? Run in such a way as to get the prize. Everyone who competes in the games goes into strict training. They do it to get a crown that will not last, but we do it to get a crown that will last forever. Therefore I do not run like someone running aimlessly; I do not fight like a boxer beating the air. No, I strike a blow to my body and make it my slave so that after I have preached to others, I myself will not be disqualified for the prize" (1 Corinthians 9:24-27).

Once again, Paul points to the prize for those of us to win in life. He says it's an eternal prize. Heaven. And because the prize is so important, Paul says we must go into training. Spiritual training.

From the tone of his words, I get the feeling Paul had a very rigorous training regimen in mind. He's not going to be a fighter throwing punches in the air. He's going to jump in the ring and let others beat on his body. That's his idea of training.

Maybe you haven't realized it, but you're in training, too. So am I. We're all being prepared to win the prize.

The chapters ahead are about that training. They lay out the regimen that God has given us in His Word. Each chapter focuses on one of nine aspects of this training plan.

I should probably tell you right up front that I was born and raised in Kentucky. And as we say in the Blue Grass state, I got myself a good ole Kentucky "edumaction." I'm a simple guy who doesn't use a lot of flowery speech to say things. I keep it real. And I keep it simple.

That's why I've labeled each aspect of this training with a word that begins with the same letter, P. It helps me keep it straight. Maybe it'll help you, too.

All of these Ps are firmly based in the truth of the Bible. Each of them could be applied to winning and losing football games, but they also apply to life. Each one has helped me to win in spite of the hardships that I've had to face.

The book is divided into two halves—like a football game. In the first half of the book, I look at the mindset of what it takes to emerge victoriously in this life. It's the internal training that precedes our action. I take a closer look at the Pain that we all must endure and how perseverance, perspective, priorities, and passion each help us emerge from the Pain victoriously.

In the second half of the book, I focus more on what it takes to be a contributing teammate on the field. I focus on your participation in the game, as well as the personnel and the practice that it takes for each of us to perform well. I then address how you can use the platform God has given you to impact the lives of others.

In addition to the two halves, there's also a pregame section with a Pregame Speech by my coach, mentor, and friend John Harbaugh. (You don't want to miss that!) And there's an overtime chapter at the end that will give you a final challenge.

I pray that God will use the book you're holding as a tool to help you understand what true winning is all about. And I pray that He'll use it to bring encouragement, challenge, and growth to your life—to help you win in spite of whatever life throws your way.

THE PREGAME
A Different Kind of Winning

*The game will begin soon. But first,
we'll step into the locker room to "hear"
a pre-game speech by Coach John Harbaugh.*

I Call Him Coach...and Friend

An introduction of John Harbaugh by David Akers

I met John Harbaugh in 1999, when he was the Special Teams Coach for the Philadelphia Eagles, and I was the Kick Off and Long Field Goal Specialist. It was my first year to play in the National Football League (NFL), and it was only John's second year as a NFL coach.

Since John was my position coach for eight years, I got to know him well. During summer two-a-days, we had a lot of time in-between practices to talk about life. We had several things in common at the time. Not only were we both new to the NFL, but we were also in very similar family situations, as well. When I started with the Eagles, neither of us had kids. But it wasn't long until we both began raising children.

We learned a lot in those early years about how to juggle our professional commitments with our family responsibilities, and we did it better some days than others.

Both on and off the field, our relationship was strong because we had a lot of trust and respect for each other. On the field, John was tough on me at times. He pushed me hard to make me the best player I could be. At times I wanted to shout, "Seriously, John! Back off a little! You're making a big deal out of nothing!" But he knew that little things are a big deal in the NFL. And sometimes in life.

We're both passionate guys, so it got a little heated at times when he'd get up in my facemask about something. But we both left those moments on the field. We'd get into a heated disagreement on game day, and then we'd laugh together at dinner the next day.

See, off the field, John was my good friend and mentor. As my coach he made me a better player. But as my friend, he made me a better man.

The reason I wanted John to write a "Pregame Speech" (some would call it a Foreword) is because he's had a major influence with my thoughts about what it means to be a winner.

He's been the head coach of the Baltimore Ravens since 2008, and he's proven himself to be a winner over and over. In just his first year

there, he led the team to the AFC championship game! And,
as I write this, he's led his team to the playoffs every year since with the
exception of one. In 2012, he won the NFL's ultimate prize—
a Super Bowl ring.

Watching from a distance, I've often thought, *C'mon, John,
you're making it look way too easy!* But it wasn't easy at all. He
was a winner in spite of a lot of roadblocks and setbacks.

By nearly every worldly standard, John Harbaugh is a
winner. But in my eyes, he's an even greater winner by a different
set of standards.

When I asked John what his definition of a winner was, his reply
had nothing to do with winning games. It wasn't about the number of
playoff games he's coached, or the Super Bowl he's won. John defines
winning with the acronym, WIN, which stands for What's Important
Now. He doesn't take his cues about what's important from the world.
He defines what's important by what God says is important in the
Bible.

Winning is about focusing on what's important to God in any
given moment of any given day. It requires listening for God's voice and
following His lead.

Here's what John told me: "We think in terms of five- and
ten-year plans—and at times, I think God does too—but sometimes God
is thinking in terms of a five- or ten-minute plan. We have to
be open to what God thinks is important at any given moment.

"Sometimes I'll be in the middle of my work," he continued, "when
a Ravens' player or staff member lets me know they have a personal need.
To God, their needs are important, so I'll stop what I'm doing and let
them know their needs are important to me, too."

I witnessed this first hand on the morning of Sunday, September 21,
2014. I awoke to a phone call from my agent telling me that my friend
and training partner, Rob Bironas, had been killed in a car accident the
night before. I was stunned.

Rob was a placekicker for the Tennessee Titans from 2005 to 2013, and he and I both lived in the Nashville area at the time of his death. We'd been kicking balls together at a local high school football field to stay in shape—hoping we'd get a call from an NFL team. His son, London, and my son, Luke, would shag balls for us as we kicked. We knew each other for about twenty years, so I felt like I was losing a good friend.

When I got the news of Rob's death, I thought: *Unbelievable! How can Rob be gone? We were just kicking together!*

I felt so bad for his wife and family. I couldn't imagine what they must be going through.

A little later that morning, I got another call. When I looked at the caller I.D. on my cell phone, I was surprised to see the name "John Harbaugh."

"Hey, John!" I answered. "What are you doing calling me on a Sunday morning. Don't you have a game in a few hours?"

"Yeah, I'm in Cleveland. We play the Browns today," he replied. "But I wanted to call and make sure you knew that Rob Bironas was killed last night in a car accident."

"Yeah, man, I just heard about it a little while ago. To be honest, I think I'm in shock."

"Well, I know you guys were good friends," John continued, "and I just wanted you to know that you're in my thoughts and prayers today. I know you're going to feel this one."

Wow, John had stepped aside from his normal pre-game routine to call and encourage me. *Who does that?*

"Man, this means the world to me that you would take time to call me this morning," I told him. "I'm really grateful!"

I really was. John defines winning as What's Important Now, and that morning, he felt like I was important. Me. God nudged him to call me, and he did. That's the kind of winner I want to be. One who defines

winning by focusing on what's important to God.
Someone who defines it in terms of what's good for other people.
Not just what's good for himself.

I've seen very few others who live like John—with such a
commitment for things that really matter. He faces life with passion and
enthusiasm. He faces adversity with mental toughness and
persistence. And he inspires the people in his life with love and encouragement. For that reason, John's name will come up several times in this
book.

And it's the reason why I asked him to write the Pregame Speech for
this book. It's not just because he's well known—
although he is. And it's not just because he's great at giving
pregame speeches—although he's the best I've ever heard!

It's because he exemplifies what this book is about.

It's Time to Go All In

by John Harbaugh

I love making pregame speeches to motivate my team. It's an important part of what head coaches do. So, I'm excited to give the "Pregame Speech" for David Akers' book, *Winning in Spite Of.*

It won't be quite the same as giving it in an NFL locker room with dozens of guys sitting around in their pads and game jerseys. And it won't be the same as it is when my adrenaline is pumping like crazy, and my mind is focused on beating our opponent. But it's still an honor to be the one who gets you pumped up for the pages ahead.

Ever since becoming the head coach of the Baltimore Ravens, I've chosen a story or hero and a theme for my team to focus on each year. In the 2014 season, I used one of the most well known Bible stories about the unbelievable faith and persistence of Noah as he built the ark. You've probably heard the story from the time you were a kid.

I think it may be the greatest faith story ever.

God told Noah to build a huge ship because there was going to be a great flood that would wipe out every living thing on earth that wasn't on the ark. Noah would have to build a floating city big enough to house two of every living creature on the planet until the flood ended.

This is not just some children's story. It really happened. Scientific discoveries lend credibility to its historical legitimacy.

Most of us can't imagine how huge of an undertaking it was for Noah and his family to build the ark. Nothing of this sort had ever been conceived of by men. After the ark, no other ship was built that big again until the nineteenth century.

God instructed Noah to build the ark out of wood. But he lived in a desert, so, where was he going to find enough lumber to build an ark that was longer than a football field? He sure couldn't run to Lowe's and put in a special order.

Tradition says Noah planted a whole forest of trees that would provide most of the wood for the ark. And then he had to nurture and grow those trees and wait decades until they grew big enough for him to cut down and saw into beams and pieces of lumber—all by hand. And that was before the real work of building the ark began!

It took unbelievable persistence and hard work for Noah to finish what God called him to do. But it took more than just Noah's persistence; it also took a team. Everyone in Noah's family participated in the project. It was a lifelong family quest. And in all, it took Noah and his family more than a century to build the ark.

It took incredible resilience, too. Can you imagine the derision Noah and his family faced from the community? They probably felt very isolated and alone; but they had each other, and they had their faith.

They had faith and guts and one another! And that carried them through to the end.

When God calls us to do something, He gives us everything we need to complete the task. And what does He ask from us in return? Our trust in Him.

Noah's life was defined by one thing. Building the ark, right? No. It was defined by his persistent, and resilient faith in God. The ark was the result.

All In and All Out

I tell my team, all the time, that if we're going to do something important, we better be ALL IN! And to be all in, you have to go ALL OUT! You have to give one hundred percent of everything you have to do the things that matter most. Just like Noah.

Everything in life that's worthwhile—including your family, your career, and your faith in God—takes hard work, commitment, perseverance, resilience, patience, and a team. Noah had all that.

Life is full of hardships and trials, so you better be ready to roll with the punches. Every time life knocks you down, you have to get back up to play another day.

In my world, your team has to outlast thirty-one other teams to win the ultimate prize—the Super Bowl trophy. (I've experienced it once in 2012, and it's one of the highlights of my life!) But there's another prize that's even more important than the Lombardi trophy. It's the ultimate prize that God has promised for those who win in life. It's Heaven. And you better believe that it takes the same kind of commitment, perseverance, resilience, patience, and teamwork to win that prize, too.

If you're going to be all in with God, you better be willing to go all out. He deserves nothing less than your best. And you know what? He wants to be with you every step of the way as you give it your all.

During the 2014 post season, my family and I went to see the movie, *Unbroken*—the story of an incredible man named Louis Zamperini, who was an Olympic athlete and World War II veteran who had to endure unbelievable hardship in a Japanese prison camp. He made it through and—later in life—went back to Japan to face and forgive the captors who treated him so cruelly when he was a prisoner.

In one scene, early in the movie, Louis's brother said something to him that was really the theme of the movie: "You can endure a moment of pain for a lifetime of glory."

It's a powerful statement, but those of us who have our eyes on the ultimate prize can take it one step further: "You can endure a lifetime of pain for an eternity of glory."

Always remember that this world isn't all there is. There is an eternal reward waiting for those of us who put our faith in Christ and overcome the trials of this life to emerge victoriously. That's the most important kind of winning any of us will ever experience.

My Super Bowl win is nothing compared to that kind of winning.

I Can't Wait

This book will take you on an incredible journey through David Akers' NFL career and his life off the field, as well. You'll be moved, inspired, challenged, and convicted as you read the pages ahead.

I've known David since 1999, and he's not only an incredible kicker, he's also an incredible husband, father, friend, and man of God. Whether you judge him by his performance on or off the field, he's a winner. I've seen David play in a lot of big games and make a lot of big kicks. And I think most anyone would look at his NFL numbers and agree that he was one of the elite kickers of his generation.

But those statistics won't tell you about his guts and never-give-up attitude. I've seen David make tackles on the best athletes in football. I've seen him change games with incredible surprise onside kicks. And I've even seen him hobble onto the field—with serious injury—to kick a make-or-break field goal at the end of a game. (He made it, and his teammates carried him to the locker room on their shoulders!)

But, what truly makes David a winner is what happened when he didn't make a big kick. It's how he responded when he blew it. He didn't duck responsibility. He manned up, owned his mistake, and got about the business of learning from it. He always worked to get better.

And another thing that makes David a winner is how he handles adversity off the field. He's had to overcome some tough times in his life, but whenever life has knocked him down, he's always gotten up to play another day.

That kind of persistence, in the midst of adversity, is what it takes to win in football. And more importantly, it's what it takes to win in life.

That's what the book you're holding is all about.

The last thing I tell my players on the Saturday night before a game is, "I can't wait to see you play tomorrow at 1:00!" Well, I have something similar to say to you.

I can't wait to see what God does in your life through this book.

– JOHN "HARBS" HARBAUGH [MARCH 2015] –

Coach John Harbaugh and me [2000].

FIRST HALF
The Right Mindset

Athletes know the importance of having the right mindset. We know that the game is not just played with our bodies; it's also played in our minds.

Whenever I missed a kick in an important game (or even in a not-so-important one), I had to go back to the sideline and clear the mistake out of my head. As my coaches would often say, I had to have a short memory.

I had to immediately get back into the right headspace and get ready to kick again. The same is true for you.

Whether you're an athlete or not, the game is often won or lost in your mind. That's where we're kicking off this book.

CHAPTER ONE

No Pain, No Gain

[Pain]

*"Gold medals aren't really made of gold.
They're made of sweat, determination,
and a hard-to-find alloy called guts."*
– DAN GABLE –

"The road to Easy Street goes through the sewer."
– JOHN MADDEN –

In 2001, my wife, Erika, and I started the David Akers Kicks for Kids Foundation. Its mission was to help poor children pursue and reach their dreams. We funded the fulfillment of all kinds of dreams—educational, economical, social, developmental, and medical.

As a part of our foundation work, I also visited a handful of local hospitals to spend time with sick children and their families. The week before Christmas in 2004, my son Luke (who was two at the time) came along with me to the Children's Hospital of Philadelphia as I read Christmas stories to some of the kids who had been admitted for long periods of time. As I was leaving the hospital that evening, I told the hospital's CEO that I was thankful Luke and I were there under those circumstances and not because he was seriously ill. That was Tuesday.

The next Sunday was Christmas Day, and Erika, Luke, and I got up early that morning and opened presents. Erika and I noticed that Luke was fussy and lethargic—and not as excited for Christmas as we thought he would be. As the morning progressed, we noticed a red spot under his eye. And before long, his eye was swelling shut. Since our doctor was out of town for Christmas, we took Luke to a local ER, where they quickly dismissed his problem as a virus that would likely clear up on its own.

But it continued to get worse. Early the next morning, I rushed him to the Children's Hospital—a forty-minute drive from our home—where we were together just days earlier. When we got there, the Children's Hospital medical staff responded very differently then they had at the first hospital we visited. They quickly diagnosed Luke's issue as cellulitis with a MRSA staph infection. And unlike the first hospital, they took it very seriously.

"This is going to get worse before it gets better," one of his doctors told us.

He was right; Luke's eyes swelled completely shut. They admitted him for what would end up being a five-day stay and gave him a very strong dose of an antibiotic that had to be mixed with chocolate so that they could just get it into his stomach.

Over the next few days, Children's Hospital doctors
closely monitored Luke's infection, and they did everything they could to
protect his sight. As we later learned, they were also
protecting his life. Erika and I were extremely impressed at how thorough
they were in assuring Luke's well-being. They treated
him as if he were their own son.

Luke walked out of the Children's Hospital five days later
with the MRSA infection under control. It was only then that the doctors
told us just how concerned they had been that the MRSA infection
would move beyond his eye and into his brain.

At that point, it would've been game over.

After experiencing how incredible the care was at Children's Hospital, we decided to focus all of our Foundation's work there. That five day
experience helped us better understand the needs
of sick children and their families.

We soon started a program called David's Locker, which assisted
families during hospital stays with items such as breathing machines,
meals, gift cards, wheelchairs, plane tickets, and computers. Anything to
make their bad situation better.

We also took part in Field of Dreams, which granted the
wishes of sick kids to attend an Eagles game, by setting them up with a
limousine for transportation, a shopping spree at the Lincoln Financial
Field team store, pregame sideline passes, and access to
a suite during the game.

And over the years, I spent dozens of hours visiting sick children and
their parents at the Children's Hospital. Most of my visits were in the
oncology center.

I enjoyed getting to know the doctors, nurses, and child-life specialists there. They were warm and gracious people. Each visit, they greeted
me with a smile, and often let me know how much they appreciated the
time I spent with patients and their families.

As an NFL player, God gave me a platform to bless others. I was merely using that platform in the oncology center of Philadelphia Children's Hospital. I found that just giving a little meant so much to families who were in a life-and-death struggle against cancer.

It was heart wrenching to see young kids with cancer, and it was almost equally as sad to watch their parents agonize over them. I couldn't imagine what it must be like to have a child with cancer. But near the end of the 2010 football season, I found out.

Standing in Their Shoes

Shortly after returning home from training camp in the summer of 2010, Erika and I started to notice that our daughter, Halley, was experiencing unusual breast growth—even though she was only five years old at the time. Halley was also a little ahead of schedule with the growth of her bone structure, so we weren't sure what to make of it.

Over the next few months, Halley's breast growth continued, and so did our concern. We took her to our doctor who determined that whatever was causing the growth seemed to be coming from her ovaries. An ultrasound revealed that her ovaries were swollen—especially her left one.

The doctor suggested we have more exams done at the Children's Hospital—the same place we took Luke. After doing some tests, our endocrinologist there wasn't too concerned. She thought it might be a cyst that would eventually disolve on its own. She told us to continue to monitor Halley and to call if anything changed.

Things did change.

The growth continued to enlarge, and our endocrinologist then recommended that Halley get an MRI. On the Friday before our 2010 season playoff game against the Packers, I took Halley to the hospital for the test. (Erika stayed home with our youngest child, Sawyer, who was two years old at the time.)

I sat alone in a waiting room for two and a half hours while Halley underwent the MRI. My mind raced in all different directions as I tried to process what was happening.

O God, please don't let this be cancer, I prayed over and over in my mind.

The radiologist was the first to look at the images, and he said there clearly was "something going on" with her ovaries, but he didn't believe it was malignant.

I took a deep breath and let out a sigh of relief.

"Thank you God!" I whispered quietly.

Still, the "something going on" was enough to cause our endocrinologist to do another ultrasound. Halley laid on the exam table still groggy from the anesthesia she was under from the MRI as she underwent the ultrasound. I watched the endocrinologist's face as she intently peered at the ultrasound screen. Her face began to show concern.

She looked up at me and said, "Something isn't right. I don't want to alarm you, but I think we need to get her to oncology right away. They need to see this."

Wham!

I knew all too well what "oncology" meant for a child her age because of all my visits to the children's hospital oncology center the past few years. I also knew what it meant for Erika and me. I'd witnessed so closely how hard children with cancer is on the parents, as well.

In less than an hour, I went from relief after the radiologist spoke to me to overwhelming fear after the endocrinologist did the ultrasound.

It felt like emotional whiplash.

Everything seemed to speed up from that time on. The nurses rolled Halley, still groggy, in a wheelchair into the oncology center.

The doctors immediately began to talk about surgery and how they weren't sure if that "something going on" was contained to her ovaries.

If I was experiencing fear before, I was now experiencing terror.

I noticed that the doctors, nurses, and child-life specialists who knew me from my previous visits were now treating me very differently. They weren't smiling at me. They weren't patting me on the shoulder. They weren't laughing and joking around. They were serious—even businesslike.

Their serious tone communicated more clearly than their words. They were treating me like the father of a cancer patient who was in a life or death battle.

Our family went to our pastor's home to have him and a few others pray for Halley. While there, I received a call from the hospital. The oncologist on the other end of the line said he thought Halley's tumor may be malignant and they needed to schedule surgery soon.

Very soon.

After listening for a few moments, I pressed him: "Are you sure it's cancerous?"

"Yes," he replied, "but the only way we can know for sure is to remove the tumor."

We scheduled the surgery for early the next week.

I felt like my whole world had come crashing down around me as I ended the call. That word "malignant" bounced around my mind the rest of the evening and made it difficult to sleep that night. I was a jumbled mess of confusion and fear.

I went to practice on Saturday and then reported to the team hotel in Philadelphia that night for Sunday's playoff game. Once again, I didn't sleep much.

Sunday morning, I attended the pregame chapel at the stadium and asked the team chaplain to pray with me. Then I dressed and went out to the field for warm-ups.

It was one of those cold and nasty winter days in Philadelphia. I went through my normal warm-up routine and kicked fairly well, but emotionally, I didn't feel right. I wasn't fully present. My mind and my heart were with my daughter.

Still, I thought my body would take over when I was called on to kick. I was counting on the muscle memory that I'd built up from years of kicking to get me through it.

Just do it like you've done it hundreds of times before, I told myself. *It's okay. You're a pro. You can do this in your sleep.*

On the game's first possession, our drive stalled at the Packers' twenty-three yard line, and our coach, Andy Reid, called on the field goal team to attempt a forty-one yarder. The ball was on the left hash, and I was kicking toward the north end zone with a fairly stiff wind blowing from the right.

I aimed right to compensate for the wind, but I kicked too much of a line drive. The ball cut through the wind and ended up wide right.

"Oh, you've got to be kidding me!" I yelled out as I tore away the chinstrap from my helmet. I was so angry! I couldn't believe I'd misjudged the wind and mishit the ball.

But it was early in the first quarter, and I figured we would have other chances. I had no idea how consequential that miss would be in the game.

Late in the second quarter, with the Packers leading 14-0, I made a short kick—from twenty-nine yards—to put our first points on the board.

Both teams scored a touchdown in the third quarter, and we were trailing 21-10 when coach called on the field goal unit again to attempt a thirty-four yarder with less than two minutes to go in the fourth quarter.

Thirty-four yards is a short kick in the NFL.

The snap was good, but the field had recently been re-sodded, and when I planted my right foot to kick, it slid forward—just past the ball—and I wrapped my foot around it. As soon as the ball left my foot, I knew I'd hit it wrong.

Once again, the kick went a little wide to the right. I missed.

No! No way! How could I miss two field goals! This is a disaster! My team was counting on me! My coaches were counting on me! All these fans were counting on me! And I blew it!

It would've been easy to blame the grass, but there was absolutely no excuse. None! I didn't miss the kick because of new sod. I missed it because my head wasn't in the game.

I should've been able to make that kick in any condition! Whenever footing is unsure, I simply make an adjustment by taking a smaller approach to the ball. It ensures that I'll get a firm plant with my right foot. I missed the kick because I didn't pay attention to the details. I wasn't focused.

We wound up losing the game to the Packers, 21-16.

Had I made those kicks, we would've advanced to the NFC divisional playoff game. But now our season was over.

As I walked off the field, I wondered if that was going to be my last game as an Eagle. It was not the way I wanted it to end. I knew I'd failed everyone in the Eagles organization and every Eagles fan.

I can't tell you how much I agonized over those kicks, knowing I'd sent seventy thousand fans home from the stadium disappointed, not to mention all the hundreds of thousands of fans who were watching on TV.

After the game, reporters asked Coach Reid if he thought my missed kicks were the reason for the loss. He simply responded, "You can do the math."

Andy was right. *Everyone* could do the math. The six points I left on the field—rather than on the scoreboard—had cost us the game and a trip to the NFC divisional playoff game.

On Monday morning, I missed the team exit meeting while Erika and I met with Halley's surgeon. By the time I made it back to the Eagles' facility for my medical checkout, the players, coaches, and trainers had all left. I went to my locker and stood in silence for a few reflective moments. This had been my "office" for twelve years. Was this my last time to stand in this familiar place?

I was in the last year of my contract with the Eagles and I had turned down the team's offer for an extension right before Christmas. I didn't think it compared favorably with what other kickers were being paid. After my two missed kicks, I figured I should go ahead and clear out my locker in case I didn't get another offer from the Eagles.

In addition, speculation of an off-season lockout had been looming in the media. I knew it would be best to get all my equipment now for off-season workouts. Just in case there was a lockout.

If this was it with the Eagles, it just didn't seem right for it to end so unceremoniously with me standing alone in front of my locker.

Is this really how it's going to end? I thought to myself as I walked out of the locker room.

For the next week, I ignored all of the media discussion and speculation about my future with the Eagles. I knew it wouldn't be good. And with Halley's surgery pending, I needed to save all my emotional energy.

A few days after the football season was over, Erika and I took Halley to the hospital for her surgery. As we stood beside her gurney in the pre-op room, we laid our hands on her and prayed earnestly. Halley didn't know what we knew, and we were trying to stay strong in front of her to hide our concern. But the more we prayed, the less we could fight back the tears. It was a powerful moment for our family.

A few minutes later, we watched the nurses roll her away to the operating room. Once they were gone, I approached the surgeon and asked if I could pray over him.

"Absolutely," he said.

I put my hand on his shoulder and cried out to God. I prayed from the deepest part of my soul that God would anoint him and guide his hands.

"God, I pray that you will use the talents you've given him for Halley's good, and help him to work with skill and precision," I started. "Make his mind sharp, and give him wisdom for whatever he encounters during the surgery. As I put my daughter's well-being into the hands of this man and his team, I'm also putting her in Your hands, God."

My voice had been quivering as I prayed, but now it was starting to crack as tears streamed down my face.

"Lord, please, please take care of Halley," I continued. "I beg of You to wipe any cancerous cells away."

The doctor said he appreciated my prayers and that he would do his best. Then he turned and headed to the operating room, while Erika and I turned the other direction and made our way to the waiting room. As we walked, everything around me was a blur, but I could feel my heart banging in my chest.

> "God places the heaviest burden on those who can handle the weight."
> - REGGIE WHITE -

I'm not sure how long Halley's surgery was, but it seemed like it dragged on for hours. I can't say I was like all those people who describe God's "peace that passes understanding" in moments like that. I could handle the pressure of a long kick for a Super Bowl win much more than I could handle the wait to find out what was happening to my daughter in the operating room.

The doctor finally came out and told us the news. He said the tumor had indeed been malignant and that it was a very rare type of cancer, especially for a child. The good news was that he was able to remove the tumor, and he believed he had contained the cancerous growth from spilling over into the surrounding tissue.

We spent that night and the next few days with Halley in her room. The hospital staff told us to make it feel as close to normal as possible in her room. So, we got a babysitter and hung out right there in her room. Unfortunately, keeping a sense of normalcy meant no visits from extended family. That was hard for all of us.

After the tumor was biopsied, the surgeon affirmed that it had been a total success. God had answered our prayers! He gave Halley the "all clear." He just asked that we continue monitoring her for signs if the cancer returned.

Thankfully, there have been no such signs.

Nine days after Halley's surgery, our family flew to Hawaii for the Pro Bowl. The stressful circumstances of Halley's cancer and my playoff loss were behind us. And the uncertainty of my future with the Eagles was before us. But God used that getaway to remind us that He had not abandoned us. And He never would.

Sadly, I never played another game for the Philadelphia Eagles. I'd played more games in an Eagles' uniform and scored more points than any other player in Eagles' history. But there was no fanfare around my departure. No pat on the back for all the field goals I'd made, or the games I'd help the team win. Not even any recognition of my long tenure in Philadelphia.

It's not how I imagined it would end with the Eagles.

Hard Times

Hard times and painful circumstances are a part of life for all of us.

Even the rich and famous can't escape pain. You may look at guys like me and think we've got it all going for us. But fame and money doesn't keep people from facing hard times. It sure hasn't for me.

Even though my NFL career has provided me a great platform for helping others, it hasn't shielded my family, or me, from the pain and suffering that comes from living in a fallen world. Far from it.

The story I just shared with you about Halley's cancer and those missed field goals were part of a string of trials that my family and I had faced from 2007 until the present. So, I've been reading a lot in the Bible about pain and suffering. And the more I read, the more I realize how big of a role it plays in our lives.

Suffering is how God shapes and reshapes our lives. If you're going through a time of suffering right now, you need to know that your trial is not unusual. And it's not meaningless if you're allowing God to work in your life through it.

"Consider it pure joy, my brothers and sisters, whenever you face trials of many kinds, because you know that the testing of your faith produces perseverance" (James 1:2-3).

Yeah, you heard it right! It says you should consider it joy when you suffer!

Joy? Really?

I don't know about you, but I'm not good at the joyful suffering thing. I know people who seem to be full of joy and peace when they suffer, but not me. I struggle with it! I usually go through trials kicking and screaming along the way.

But eventually I come to my senses and realize that God is in control—despite how circumstances appear. I know that God is walking through the trial with me—even if I don't always see Him there. And that God is doing a good work in me through the pain— even if I don't understand what it is at the time.

When we're going through hardship, it can seem like God has abandoned us. But the opposite is true. The fact that God allows us to go through pain is actually a sign that He loves us and wants the best for us.

"Endure hardship as discipline; God is treating you as sons. For what son is not disciplined by his father? If you are not disciplined (and everyone undergoes discipline), then you are illegitimate children and not true sons. Moreover, we have all had human fathers who disciplined us and we respected them for it. How much more should we submit to the Father of our spirits and live!...No discipline seem pleasant at the time, but painful. Later on, however, it produces a harvest of righteousness and peace for those who have been trained by it" (Hebrews 12:7-9,11).

When God let's us go through hardship, He's treating us like His children. So, suffering is evidence that you're His son or daughter.

Thanks to the Holy Spirit's patient work in my life, and the help of some good friends, I'm learning that suffering is not just a part of my life. It's an *important* part of it.

The Apostle Paul knew how important it is. That's why he once said, *"I delight in weaknesses, in insults, in hardships, in persecutions, in difficulties"* (2 Corinthians 12:10).

And it's why he also said: *"We also rejoice in our sufferings, because we know that suffering produces perseverance; perseverance, character; and character, hope"* (Romans 5:3-4).

Is this guy for real? God delights in hardship? He rejoices in suffering?

Yep. Paul knew that suffering is important because it matures us. It builds perseverance, character, and hope in us. It makes us more like Jesus.

Winning in Spite Of

I believe the only way we can win in spite of the hardship in our lives is to endure it and learn from it.

If you give up in the middle of your trial, you lose.

"You're never a loser until you quit trying."
— MIKE DITKA —

But if you keep going until the end, you receive the prize that's in store for those who persevere. At times, you'll fall down—we all do—but the difference between winning and losing is whether or not you stay down.

I'm a big fan of Sylvester Stallone's Rocky movies that were popular in the seventies, eighties, and nineties. I can relate to them because of their connection with blue-collar life in Philadelphia, where I spent so much of my NFL career.

I love that triumphant sequence in the first *Rocky* movie where he slowly gets in shape by beating on the sides of beef in a meat locker and running through the streets of Philly in his gray sweats (with the building momentum of the *Rocky* theme song playing in the background), and finally has his triumphant moment running up the seventy-two steps of the Philadelphia Museum of Art.

In 1980, they immortalized that scene by putting up a life-size bronze statue of Rocky at the top of the steps. The *Rocky* statue and the "Rocky Steps" are two of the biggest tourist sites in Philadelphia.

Rocky and his hardened Philadelphia way of life are the way I want to live when it comes to how I handle hard times.

I love a line from *Rocky Balboa*, the movie that Stallone made later in his career—long after the original five movies he made in his prime. The quote comes from a part of the movie where Rocky (Stal-

lone) is talking to his son, who resents him and his attempt
to make a boxing comeback. It's a profound and poignant moment in
the film:

"Let me tell you something you already know. The world ain't all sunshine and rainbows. It's a very mean and nasty place, and I don't care how tough you are, it will beat you to your knees and keep you there permanently if you let it. You, me, or nobody is going to hit as hard as life. But it ain't about how hard you hit. It is about how hard you can get hit and keep moving forward—how much you can take and keep moving forward. That's how winning is done!"

If life has knocked you down, get back up. And when it knocks you
down again, get back up again.

Cause that's how winning is done. And that's what this
book is about.

"Adversity causes some men to break
and others to break records."
- ARTHUR WARD -

*Brochure for **Kicks for Kids** program showing my locker [2003].*

CHAPTER TWO

Never Give Up!

[Perseverance]

"Never give up! Failure and rejection are
only the first step to succeeding."

— JIM VALVANO —

---

*"If you're trying to achieve, there will
be roadblocks.... If you run into a wall, don't
turn around and give up. Figure out how to
climb it, go through it, or work around it."*

— MICHAEL JORDAN —

I was ready to quit before I made my first NFL field goal.

After finishing my college football days at the University of Louisville, I hoped to get selected in the 1997 NFL draft. The draft back then wasn't the same as it is today. It wasn't the five day, over-the-top, prime time show like it is now. It all happened over two days.

Late in the draft, the Pittsburgh Steelers called to tell me it looked like I might be their last pick. I was so pumped because very few kickers get drafted. Most teams wait until after the draft and sign a kicker as a free agent.

My heart was in my throat. *Is this really happening?*

I waited anxiously for the Steeler's turn to arrive while other teams made their final picks.

C'mon, hurry up! I've waited long enough for this moment!

Finally, Pittsburgh was on the clock and I could imagine its coaches in the war room confirming me as their final choice. Soon the NFL rep stepped up to the podium with their pick. I listened closely to hear my name. My eyes were focused on the bottom of my bubble-screen TV to see my name crawl across it.

This was going to be an once-in-a-lifetime experience.

The NFL rep cleared his throat. "With the two hundred and twenty-third pick of the 1997 NFL draft, the Pittsburgh Steelers select…"

At this point, he paused. They always leave a dramatic pause when they get to the name, but this time it was longer than ever!

C'mon already, just say it!

"Mike Adams from the University of Texas."

"Are you kidding me?" I blurted out without thinking. "Did he just say *Mike Adams*? Did *that* just happen?"

Seventeen more players were chosen before the 1997 draft concluded, and not one was a left-footed kicker from the University of Louisville.

I would have to enter the NFL as an undrafted free agent. Or, let's call it what it really is: a glorified walk-on.

It was a pretty big letdown, but I knew it wasn't the end of the world. Like I said, it's more common for kickers to not get drafted. But I also knew the chances of making an active roster had just dropped dramatically.

The Carolina Panthers called me less than a week after the draft to offer me a tryout at their summer training camp. I accepted their offer, even though I knew my chance of making their cut was slim. The Panthers already had one of the best kickers in the NFL, John Kasey, who had just come off a Pro Bowl year where he'd led the league in field goals made.

When teams have an established kicker, they'll often bring another kicker into camp to cut down the workload on their number-one guy. (It's what's known as a "camp leg.") It also provides insurance in case the primary kicker gets injured.

Still, I was excited to be there. It was my first training camp experience, and I hoped to learn a lot from one of the best during my short time with the Panthers. Kasey spent a lot of time helping me identify the flaws in my kicking technique. I totally changed my kicking form that summer.

As expected, the Panthers released me after I played in their third preseason game. So, I returned to Kentucky and took a job as a permanent substitute teacher. I also continued to practice my kicking form—using a lot of what I'd learned from Kasey.

Then I spent three months in the early spring of 1998 at Vero Beach, Florida, training with kicking instructor Doug Blevins—in hopes that I'd get a call from another team that season. But that call didn't come until late spring of the next year when the Atlanta Falcons wanted to sign me to their preseason roster. I accepted their invitation, but once again, I knew it was a long shot. Like the Panthers, the Falcons had an established kicker, Morten Andersen, who was also one of the best in the league. (One of the best of all time, for that matter.) He was a seven-time Pro Bowler who was entering his seventeenth season at the time. (He ended up playing twenty-five seasons and didn't stop until he was forty-seven!)

This time, Erika and I decided to move to Atlanta so I could immerse myself with the team. I was there for a majority of the off-season training camp.

Once again, I valued the time of learning from a seasoned veteran.

I thought, *If I could only have half the career that Morten Andersen has, I'd be ecstatic. Shoot, I'd even be ecstatic if I were to have a quarter of the career he's had!*

Andersen was very willing to share his veteran insights. He taught me a lot about what a true professional does to prepare his body in the offseason. And he modeled how I should push myself to get better and better.

I owe a lot to both Andersen and Kasey. They taught me things I used the rest of my career.

At the close of training camp, the Falcons told me they were impressed with my kicking, and they discussed with me the possibility of being on their practice squad. The practice squad, at that time, was five guys that all teams kept on beyond their regular roster to develop for the future. (Currently, the practice squad is made up of eight guys.)

It meant they thought I had NFL potential. But they told me they'd have to go through the procedural move of first releasing me from their roster before they'd be able to sign me to their practice squad.

As soon as the Falcons released me, another team called my agent and told him they, too, would like to sign me to their practice squad. It was the Washington Redskins. I knew their kicker situation wasn't nearly as good as the Falcons, so I thought I'd have a much better chance of being promoted to their fifty-three men roster.

I chose to sign with the Redskins instead of the Falcons.

It turned out to be a good move. Going into the third week of the season, my long-awaited opportunity came when the Redskins waived their kicker and moved me on to their active roster.

I'd finally made it to the big league! This was my "Jerry Maguire" moment!

Show me the money, Jerry! Show me the "kwan!"

The next week, I joined the team on a road trip to Seattle where we played the Seahawks in the Kingdome. I couldn't believe it!

I get to start my career by kicking in a dome? Yes! Man, this is going to be awesome!

It was my chance—maybe my only chance—to show the Redskins, and every other pro team, what I could do.

I kicked off my career by kicking off that game. The kick was high and a bit short. The Seahawks return man, Steve Broussard, fielded it at the 10-yard line. He hit it up the middle, busted through a hole in our defense and emerged untouched. He then cut toward the sideline to my left where he had open field in front of him.

Now, I like to think of myself as having better than average speed—especially early in my career. I started out as a soccer player in high school before switching to football, and once I made the switch, I had a lot of experience running down return men in high school and college. No one had ever returned one of my kickoffs for a touchdown.

Not until that day.

I timed my angle like I had so many times before to catch Broussard as he ran up the sideline. It would be my first NFL tackle. Except, when I got there, Broussard had already been there and left. He was leaving me in the dust!

I could hear in my mind ESPN legend Chris "Boomer" Berman saying in his staccato voice, "He could go all the way!"

And he did! Ninety yards for a touchdown.

What? Are you kidding me? My first kickoff returned for a touchdown!

It wasn't how I'd planned the start off my career. I guess it was my rude awakening that the speed of the game in the NFL is much faster than at the college level.

Welcome to the NFL, right?

Back on the sideline, I kept telling myself to calm down. *Just relax and do what you do.*

If only that had been the sole lowlight of the day. But it wasn't.

After we scored our first touchdown, I made the extra point. My ensuing kick off was worse than the first one. I only kicked it to the fifteen yard line. But on the bright side, this one wasn't returned for a touchdown.

My first field goal attempt was a nice short one to start my career, right? Wrong. It was nearly a fifty-yarder. I lined up and gave it a shot. I felt like I hit it well, but the ball drew to the right, and I missed the field goal by less than a foot.

I was so upset with myself. *You've got to be kidding me! I'm really blowing this!*

I had a second field goal attempt that half, and this one was from forty-eight-and-a-half yards out—only a yard shorter than my first attempt.

I knew I had to correct some from my last kick, so I pushed this one a little to the left. And this time I missed it to the left!

Great job, Dave! Way to over-correct and absolutely blow it!

The first half was a disaster. I was too pumped up, and I was pressing too hard to perform well. As a result, I was performing horribly!

After halftime, I didn't see much action until late in the

fourth quarter when we cut the Seahawks lead to 24-14. Our coach decided to go for an onside kick. This was my chance to redeem myself, at least a little. A well-placed onside kick could put us back in the game.

I *did* place the kick well, but unfortunately, the Seahawks recovered it, and it was game over—for the team and for me.

To recap my NFL debut: I kicked two short kickoffs—with one returned for a touchdown. I had two field goal attempts and missed one to the right and one to the left. And I wasn't able to convert on a critical onside kick.

Not surprisingly, the Redskins handed me my walking papers two days later.

I felt like a total failure. I knew I'd had little chance of making the cut with Carolina and Atlanta, but this opportunity was different. I was the starter. It was my job to win.

And I didn't.

At that point, I was ready to call it quits. I felt like my career was over before it had really begun. I had one shot, and I blew it.

Even before the Redskins officially released me, I began to pack my truck with what little belongings I had with me. I knew what was coming, so when it came, I was able to leave D.C. for home the same day.

As I crossed the border into Virginia, I called Erika on my cell phone.

"I'm going to quit and move on," I dejectedly told her. "I've got to do what's best for us."

She and I had only been married for just more than a year, and I felt like it was time for me to be a better provider. She had been an amazing wife. She'd made countless sacrifices because she knew how important it was to me to be an NFL player. It was my dream, and she wanted to do everything she could to support it.

She had worked to pay the bills while I took lower-paying jobs as a substitute teacher and waiter at a steakhouse in-between my NFL opportunities. Not only that, she'd cashed in a savings bond her grandparents had given her when she was a child to pay for my training with Doug Blevins.

She had been without her husband weeks and months at a time while I attended training camps and trained with Blevins. And she had already put her desires to start a family on hold because things in our lives were so unstable and our future was so unpredictable, at that point.

Before I made the call, I thought about how just a week before she'd driven my pick-up truck up from Atlanta so I could drive each day to the Redskins practice facility. Now, I was in the same truck making the exact opposite drive home. All I could think was, *What a loser!*

I told Erika it was time to stop chasing my NFL dream and become the husband she deserved. It startled me when she disagreed.

She told me I should keep going after it. I should keep trying. I shouldn't give up. That's what she wanted and deserved from her husband.

> *"My motto was always to keep swinging. Whether I was in a slump or feeling badly or having trouble off the field, the only thing to do was keep swinging."*
> — HANK AARON

Knowing that I needed more than just a pep talk, Erika reminded me of a tip I'd received from Doug Pelfrey, who kicked for the Cincinnati Bengals at the time and had played for the University of Kentucky, which is in my hometown, Lexington.

"Doug told you that it takes three to four years for an undrafted kicker to get established in the NFL," she pronounced. "You've only been at it for two years, and you've only had one game experience. I think you need to give it one more year. Then, if it doesn't work out, you can quit with no regrets."

I immediately knew she was right. After a long pause, I replied, "Okay, one more year."

Less than four months later, the Philadelphia Eagles offered me a contract.

Hang in There

For me, there's been no greater tool for winning, in spite of my failure and suffering, than perseverance.

Perseverance is a resolve to keep going in the midst of difficulties—or when success is delayed. It's hanging on when life gets really hard.

It's not giving up.

I grew up in the Michael Jordan era of the NBA. Jordan is arguably the best basketball player ever. His Chicago Bulls teams won six NBA championships and probably would've won more had Jordan not stepped away from basketball for a few years, in his prime, to try his hand at professional baseball. He's also the fourth leading scorer of all time in the NBA, and he scored more than sixty points in a game five times. Only Wilt Chamberlain has done it more.

And, yet, Jordan is the first to admit that he's missed a whole lot of shots. And some of them were important shots.

In a Nike TV commercial, Jordan once said, "I've missed more than nine thousand shots in my career. I've lost more than three hundred games. Twenty-six times, I've been trusted to take the game winning shot and missed. I've failed over and over again in my life. And that is why I succeed."

Translation: Jordan attributes his success to not giving up, even though he failed a lot.

That's perseverance.

Rub Some Dirt on It

Pain is for a season. And failure is only temporary. If we keep going, we'll get to the other side of it.

But as spiritual as that sounds, it's not that easy. Not for me it isn't.

I think the hardest thing in the world (when I'm in the midst of a trial) is to think about the future. Most of us can't get past the pain we're feeling in the moment, and all we want to do is throw in the towel. That's a normal feeling for all of us.

But we can't quit.

Men, it doesn't matter how we feel when we're going through a trial. We have to man up, not give up—especially those of us who have a wife and children who are counting on us. I know it's not easy. I know it's a huge struggle. Trust me, I've picked myself up off the ground many times.

But I can't sugar coat it for myself—so I won't sugar coat it for you, either. If you're lying on the ground, crying about your circumstances, stop it. Get up and keep going.

Suffering and failure are a part of life, and whining and complaining about it doesn't change your circumstances.

When I was a kid, I'd sometimes fall down and get hurt—and then I'd run crying to my dad. After checking me out, he'd look me in the eye and say this phrase: "Get back up and rub some dirt on it. It'll be fine."

Maybe you've heard that phrase come out of your dad's mouth, too.

It always sounded rude and uncaring at the time, but like all good parents, my dad was preparing me for real life—where you have to get up every time you fall down. And as much as I wanted to lie on the ground and moan about it, my dad knew that just lying there wouldn't make the pain go away.

Sometimes we just need to man up and do what our dad's told us to do: Get up, rub some dirt on it, and keep going.

Now, I still don't know what good it does to rub dirt on it, but it sure sounds like the manly thing to do. For all I care, you can get up and wipe the dirt off before you keep going. All that matters is that you get up. And keep going. Every time you fall.

Again, and again, and again.

"A champion is someone who gets up when he can't."
- JACK DEMPSEY -

Big Waves

One of the perks of going to the Pro Bowl was getting an all-expenses-paid trip to Hawaii. The NFL housed players at the Ko Olina Resort on the island of Oahu. The resort is not far from the ocean.

During several of my Pro Bowl getaways to Hawaii, I got to boogie board. Man, did the waves pound me! Hawaii waves aren't like mainland ocean waves. They're huge!

At first, I really enjoyed getting knocked around by them. When I'd fall off my board from the top of a wave, I'd then fight to get back to the surface for a breath of air. I would hop right back on the board and search for the next big wave.

Here it comes. And there I go on another ride!

I would do this over and over for hours.

I was the same way as a kid. When my family would go to the beach, my parents would have to drag me out of the water. As a child, I never seemed to run out of energy. When one wave knocked me down, I'd jump right up to battle the next cresting wave. Over, and over, and over, and over again. For me, the only bad part about going to the beach was that, sooner or later, I'd have to go home.

I guess I'm still a water rat. But as an adult, I seem to run out of energy quicker.

Now, when I get tired of the constant pounding of the waves, I make my way to the warmth of the beach and recharge in the tropical sunshine.

At the Ko Olina Resort, there was a lagoon that was blocked off from the ocean waves by a pile of big rocks. I loved going to that lagoon to float on calm waters as I soaked in the sunshine. It was a restful break from fighting the waves on the beach.

The ocean waves remind me of the hardships that have continued to come at my family and me the past seven years. At times, they've been relentless and overwhelming. Just when we felt like we were starting to get back on our feet from one wave, another would hit us. Sometimes it even felt like several waves were hitting us at once!

Many times, I've been exhausted by the waves of hardship, and I've wanted to make my way back up on the beach to rest in the sun. Or take a stroll along the beach at the edge of the surf and just let the shallow waves roll over my feet. Or float around peacefully on the calm waters of the lagoon. That would be really nice.

We've been hit by a lot of different waves, including: losing millions of dollars, surviving Halley's cancer, dealing with miscarriages, helping Luke battle health issues, dealing with my own chronic abdominal and groin pain, grappling with the failure of missed kicks, struggling with depression, twice losing my job and uprooting to a completely different part of the country, getting pounded

by the media, and on several occasions, even getting
death threats from fans. I could go on, but you get the picture.

Sometimes the waves are relentless.

Sometimes they're big, and sometimes they're smaller.

And sometimes it seems like they just keep coming.

To be honest, there have been some good times in between. But
when hardship comes in waves, it wears you down. It gets harder and
harder to rise to the occasion—to get back up on your feet.

I've often cried out to God, begging Him to allow me to
recharge in peace for a while and grow in the rays of His Son.

I need some rest, Lord! I need to experience some calmer waters!

But often, the peace doesn't come in the form of calmer waters. It
comes from the quieting work He does in the deeper parts of my soul—
even as the waves keep crashing around me.

If you've been there, you know what I mean. If you're there now,
you're probably tired of the waves. You're probably exhausted. And you
may be ready to give up.

Don't.

"Persistence can change failure into extraordinary achievement."

– MATT BIONDI –

God has given me the strength to get back up when I thought
I couldn't take another step. And He'll give you the strength to do the
same thing.

God hasn't abandoned you, and He's not being cruel. He's making
you more pure in your love for Him. He's making you more dependent
on Him. He's making you more like Him.

So, get back up and rub some dirt on it. It'll be fine.

The Extra Point:

When I was ready to give up my NFL dream in 1997, Erika's words of encouragement kept me going. Her words carried more weight in my life than anybody's. And her encouragement kept me going like nothing else could.

We all need an "Erika" or two to help us stay in the game. We all need their words of encouragement and their willingness to walk through the painful trial with us.

Several times, the writer of Hebrews calls us to encourage one another because life can be difficult.

"But **encourage one another daily**, as long as it is called 'Today,' so that none of you may be hardened by sin's deceitfulness" (Hebrews 3:13, emphasis added).

"Let us **hold unswervingly** to the hope we profess, for he who promised is faithful. And let us consider how we may **spur one another** on toward love and good deeds. Let us not give up meeting together, as some are in the habit of doing, but let us **encourage one another**—and all the more as you see the Day approaching" (Hebrews 10:23-25, emphasis added).

Our encouragement can help others persevere when times get hard. Just like their encouragement can help us persevere.

The literal meaning of the word *encouragement* is, "to empower with courage." When we go through trials, it's easy to lose our courage. That's why we need others to "empower us with courage" through their words and actions.

Just like Erika did for me.

"A friend loves at all times, and a brother is born for adversity" (Proverbs 17:17).

So, who are the Erika's in your life? Who is it that you can trust to encourage you when everything is falling a part.

Likewise, are you a person others can trust to encourage them when life is hard?

2002 Pro Bowl with Donovan McNabb

2012 Pro Bowl with Patrick Willis and my family

The calm lagoon serving as a respite from the powerful waves at the Ko Olina Ihilini resort.

CHAPTER THREE

Whose Got It Better Than Us?

[Perspective]

---

*"You can't always control circumstances.
However, you can always control your attitude,
approach, and response. Your options are to complain
or to look ahead and figure out how to make the
situation better."*

– TONY DUNGY –

---

*"I'm just thankful for everything, all the
blessings in my life.... I think that's the best way
to start your day and finish your day. It keeps
everything in perspective."*

– TIM TEBOW –

You're probably already thinking it, so I'll go ahead and say it: pro football players make a lot of money. It's true. I'm very thankful for every dollar I made during my time in the NFL.

But pro football players have another reality. We have a very short window of our lives in which we can earn that kind of money. Some keep their celebrity status after their football careers by working as analysts in the media, but most players' lives become a lot more ordinary after they retire—and so do their salaries.

NFL players joke that the NFL stands for "Not For Long." It's true. The average NFL player has a career of just over three years. I was fortunate that my career lasted five times longer than the average.

All through my time in the NFL, I assumed that the money I was making would have to supplement my family's income for the rest of our lives. For that reason, I managed my money very carefully.

First of all, I wanted to be a good steward of what God had given us. Second, I wanted to be very generous with others who were in need. And third, I wanted to invest wisely for the future.

I invested much of my income with Wachovia Securities for the early part of my career. I grew to trust my investment team there, and I invested most of my money in the securities that they advised.

But in the fall of 2006, an ex-teammate told me about an investment company out of Austin, Texas, called Triton Financial. He and his brother—a man I respected a lot—worked for Triton, and they were both investing their money there, as well. I had my Wachovia team look over the fundamentals of Triton's investment opportunities, and I knew other players who were having their financial guys do the same. Everything checked out. Our advisors concurred that Triton looked fundamentally sound and had a game plan to grow a portfolio in a safe and modest way.

You know the old adage, "If it looks too good to be true, it probably is." That did not apply to Triton. It was solid and conservative. Just what I wanted.

I started slowly transferring my investment money into Triton over the next few years. Then I sold a piece of property that we owned and invested the proceeds into Triton, as well.

When the bottom fell out of the market in 2008, my financial team left Wachovia for another company. To that point, we were very pleased with the way Triton had been producing for us. Just before the collapse, Triton's CEO, Kurt Barton, advised me to get rid of some stock that he thought was going to get smashed in the coming market collapse. Fortunately, I did. Just weeks later that stock bottomed out.

After that, my confidence in Triton was very strong. So, instead of following my investment team to another company, I pulled all my money out of other investments and put it into Triton.

It made sense to me at the time. Triton was continually growing, and they had just struck a deal to partner with Fidelity Investments. And heck, everyone trusts Fidelity! Follow the green line, right? I was receiving monthly statements from both Fidelity and Triton, and they both said the same thing—our portfolio was growing.

Triton had another company with a long history and a great reputation vouching for it.

I was so thankful for Triton. My money was in good hands, and I slept well at night knowing that I was getting a good and safe return that would take care of us long after my NFL career was over.

I was playing for Philadelphia at the time, and we were living in Medford, New Jersey. We were feeling optimistic about my career and our financial situation, so Erika and I decided to buy land and build our dream home in North Carolina. It was a home we could raise our kids in, and it could be another investment for the future. We were intentionally buying it in an area where real estate values would likely increase.

But we weren't just looking out for ourselves. Through the help of local pastors and my Kicks for Kids Foundation, we identified twenty families in the Medford area who were in financial need. We committed to give more than eighty thousand dollars to help these families get back on their feet.

Then the bottom fell out.

In December 2009, I got a call from an FBI agent. As you probably already know, it's never good to get a call from the FBI! Most likely it means either you've done something wrong or someone's done something wrong to you. In my case, it was the latter.

It turned out I was wrong about Triton. The FBI agent told me Triton Financial was being taken over by the SEC and put into receivership. I wasn't exactly sure what he was talking about. To me, SEC stood for the Southeastern Conference—you know, the powerful college football conference that boasts Alabama, LSU, Tennessee, Ole Miss, and Florida (oh, and my hometown University of Kentucky Wildcats, who is an SEC basketball powerhouse). But the agent clarified that he was talking about the Securities and Exchange Commission, and that Triton had been running a Ponzi scheme. Okay, of course I knew about *that* SEC, too, but I never thought I'd ever have any interaction with them!

Triton had bilked their investors out of millions of dollars, and I was one of those investors. The more I learned from the FBI agent, the more I was stunned into silence. I had invested eight out of eleven year's worth of my NFL salary with Triton.

To make it a little clearer, I had invested *four million dollars* in Triton's Ponzi scheme.

Four million dollars!

Our family's nest egg!

And it was all gone!

No! How can this be happening! We've lost almost all the money we have!

This is a nightmare! How am I ever going to recoup this?

The fact is we couldn't recoup it. It was gone.

I can't find the words to tell you how I felt. I kept thinking how I'd been so careful to put away most of my income for the future—and now it was gone. All I can do to help you understand is to ask you to imagine how you would feel if you lost four million dollars.

I was struggling to comprehend it. But after grappling for a while with the gravity of the situation, my next thought was how the news was going to affect Erika.

How am I going to tell my wife?

This was one of several moments in my life when I felt like a failure. Only this time, I wasn't letting down my team or our fans with a missed kick. It was much closer to home than that. I was letting down my wife and kids. And I also felt like I'd let down my parents, because they, too, had invested in Triton on my positive recommendation.

I procrastinated telling Erika about the loss, but she knew something was wrong with me. (Wives have an intuitive ability to sense when there's something wrong with their husbands! It's hard to hide anything from them. Am I right, guys?)

"David, what is wrong with you?" she kept asking. But I kept dodging her question. Until one day, as we were talking in the kitchen, she looked me straight in the eyes and asked that question again. But this time, her tone let me know she wasn't going to take "I'm fine" as an answer.

I looked down at the countertop I was leaning against and mustered up the courage to tell her what had happened. I was physically weak and *actually* needed the stability of the countertop for support.

"Babe, I'm so sorry to have to tell you this," I started, "but umm… umm…it's all gone. We've lost almost everything! Triton has cheated us out of our life's savings!"

Erika was silent for a moment, so I tried to read her face to see what she was feeling. To my surprise, she didn't look angry or horrified.

She looked relieved.

"David, I was so scared," she said as she let out a sigh. "I thought you were going to tell me that you've been having an affair."

She paused and added, "I thought you were going to tell me you had cheated on me."

Erika's response surprised and astonished me. I felt like I was seeing our wedding vows played out in front of me. For better or for worse. For richer or for poorer. For as long as we both shall live. I now knew that she truly loved me—for me and not for my money.

Erika helped me see our financial loss in a different way. I'd been feeling like a failure as a husband because I'd lost our savings in a bad investment deal. But Erika was relieved that I hadn't had an affair.

What a shift in perspective!

The Shift

I learned a lot from losing four million dollars. For one thing, I learned that you *couldn't* always control circumstances. But you can control your perspective on them.

Sometimes, shifting your perspective on your situation is the key to *winning in spite of* it. If you keep your focus on the pain and hardship, you may find yourself going into a tailspin of confusion and despair. But sometimes, shifting your perspective can actually pull you out of your tailspin.

Of course, controlling your perspective is easier said than done. More times than not, I've let hardship affect how I viewed my life and myself. If circumstances are good, then it's easy to think that life is good, and God is good—and just maybe, I'm good, too. But when circumstances go bad—like four million dollars worth of bad—it's hard to see that anything in life is good. At that moment, everything stinks.

That's when I have to change my perspective. It's no different for you.

When you shift your perspective, you compare your current situation with something equally or more important that's going well. Erika and I were able to rise above our financial loss partly because we compared our finances (something important) with our marriage (something much more important). And it paled in comparison.

Erika knew our marriage could weather a financial loss, but an affair was a whole different story. And she helped me see our financial loss from *that* perspective.

Don't get me wrong, it was very hard to see that money disappear—it still is—but it has brought Erika and I closer, and it's made us a lot more dependent on God.

It reminds me of a family motto about perspective that John Harbaugh often shares with the players he coaches.

"Who has it better than us?" he passionately yells. "*Nobody!*"

He said it a number of times when he was one of my coaches in Philadelphia. He wanted to remind us that, despite our hardships, we had it good. Very good. We got to do what we loved for a living—and we got paid well for it.

John told me that his dad, Jack, would repeat that family motto during a time in their lives when they didn't have much. Jack was also a college football coach. (In fact, he was almost *my* coach because I considered playing for him at Western Kentucky before choosing Louisville.) He used to share that motto with John, his brother Jim (who was my head coach when I played for the 49ers), and the rest of his family—long before any of them were earning a big NFL salary.

Even when the Harbaugh family had to go without the things they wanted (and sometimes needed), they chose the perspective that nobody had it better than them. *Nobody.*

That was the perspective Erika and I chose after losing our life's savings, and it made all the difference in how we saw our lives. We saw ourselves as blessed rather than cursed.

How would it change your life if you chose that perspective despite what you're going through?

From Saul to Paul

The Apostle Paul knew all about shifting perspectives—and how it changes everything.

"Saul was uttering threats with every breath and was eager to kill the Lord's followers. So he went to the high priest. He requested letters addressed to the synagogues in Damascus, asking for their cooperation in the arrest of any followers of the Way he found there. He wanted to bring them—both men and women—back to Jerusalem in chains. As he was approaching Damascus on this mission, a light from heaven suddenly shonedown around him. He fell to the ground and heard a voice saying to him, 'Saul! Saul! Why are you persecuting me?'

'Who are you, lord?' Saul asked.

And the voice replied, 'I am Jesus, the one you are persecuting! Now get up and go into the city, and you will be told what you must do.'

The men with Saul stood speechless, for they heard the sound of someone's voice but saw no one! Saul picked himself up off the ground, but when he opened his eyes, he was blind. So his companions led him by the hand to Damascus. He remained there blind for three days and did not eat or drink" (Acts 9:1-9, NLT).

Later in the story, God asked a disciple named Ananias to go pray over Saul to receive his sight back. But if I'm Ananias, I'm saying, "Whoa! Hold on! You want me to do what? Don't you know Saul is a notorious Christian killer?"

But God made it clear to Ananias that Saul was going to do a one hundred eighty degree turn from killing Christians to converting people into Christians.

Talk about a shift in perspective!

The shift is so strong that Saul changed his name to Paul *(see Acts 13:9)*. Some believe his name change was to mark the separation of his former life with his new life. But others think he traded in his Hebrew name (Saul) for a Gentile name (Paul). In other words, this guy, who was the most legalistic kind of Jew, was now going to associate himself with the Gentiles so he could take the Good News to them.

Either way, Paul's name change is symbolic of his radical perspective change. From Judaism to Christianity. From killing to converting. From legalism to grace.

This is a big deal because when Paul's perspective changed, so did his beliefs, his attitudes, his values, his words, and his actions. Everything!

Are you tracking with me? A change in your perspective can change everything about your life! Especially when the change causes you to focus on God. It did for Paul. And it did for me. If God can change Saul into Paul (both his name and his heart), what can he do with you and me?

I operated from a worldly point of view for most of my life. I believed in God, but I didn't know Him—and I surely didn't know much about His Word because I hated to read. I mean I *really* hated to read! But in 1999, I started to shift my focus to God, rather than on everything else in my life.

I began to read His Word, and my perspective changed radically. Just like Paul's did. It didn't change my name, but it changed just about everything else. My beliefs. My attitudes. My values. My words. And ultimately my actions.

I began to live in a way where my actions resembled more

of what I said I believed. If I was going to call myself a Christian, I decided I needed to walk the walk, not just talk the talk. And I set out to do so.

My change in perspective resembled Paul's change. Later in his life, Paul described it this way:

"But whatever were gains to me, I now consider loss for the sake of Christ. What is more, I consider everything a loss because of the surpassing worth of knowing Christ Jesus my Lord, for whose sake I have lost all things. I consider them garbage that I may gain Christ and be found in him, not having a righteousness of my own that comes from the law, but that which is through faith in Christ— the righteousness that comes from God on the basis of faith" (Philippians 3:7-9).

Garbage is a strong word. When I think of garbage, I think of a pile of foul, putrid, useless items that need to be thrown out and disposed of. Another version of the Bible translates the same word as *dung*, instead of *garbage*. That's an even stronger word!

Paul is saying that the stuff he previously considered great, he now considers crap! Why? Because he's focused on something so much better—the prize.

He's focused on Heaven.

That's what I want my focus to be on as well. How about you?

In the Storm

One of the things that affect the way we feel about our circumstances is whether or not we truly believe and recognize that God is involved in them. We worry when we don't see God's presence in our trials. And we fear the future when we don't envision God in it.

Life can be terrifying even when things are going well because you never know what's around the corner.

I couldn't predict that Halley was going to have to fight a
battle against cancer or that Triton was going to cheat me out of millions.
(If I could've predicted it, I wouldn't have trusted them
with my money!)

It's the same for you. You can be walking on top of the world one
minute and it can roll over and crush you the next.

Your health can be great one day, and not long afterward,
you can find yourself battling an incurable disease—even though
you eat right and work out.

Things can be great with your spouse (or significant other) one day,
and not long afterward, you can find out he or she has been cheating on
you—even though you've been faithful yourself.

You can be in the prime of your career one day, and not
long afterward, you find out your company has laid you off
for reasons beyond your control—even though you performed well
for your employer.

For football players, we live with the constant possibility of
getting cut or traded. We're only as good as our last game. I had
a Pro Bowl season my first year with San Francisco and then was
released after the second year because of a chronic injury in my
kicking leg that affected my performance. What a difference
a year makes!

We can only stay positive about the looming potential for things to
go bad by understanding that God is in control, and we need Him *all the
time*—whether life is easy or hard.

I don't know about you, but sometimes I find it a lot easier to trust
in myself and in others more than in God. But, come on. Do we really
think we can handle things better than God?

When Jesus walked the earth, one of His greatest miracles was
calming the storm. (He has so much control that even the weather
obeys Him!) One time, the disciples were terrified in their boat as it
was tossed around in a storm. They thought they were going to die.

Then Jesus appeared near their boat walking on the water. And in an amazing act of faith, Peter jumped out of the boat and began to walk to Jesus on water, too.

Hold on for a second! It's amazing enough that Jesus was walking on water, but Peter? He wasn't always the most spiritual guy, but he actually walked a few steps on the waves! But then he started to look around at the storm—the relentless winds, the dangerous lightning, the pounding thunder, the torrential rain, and the crashing waves. His faith started lagging—can you blame him? And before Peter knew it, he was sinking.

So what did Peter do? He changed his perspective!

He took his eyes off the storm and looked back at Jesus. He cried out to Jesus to save him, and Jesus did.

We can probably learn a lot of other things from that story, but here's the point I'm making: When Peter shifted his perspective from the storm to Jesus, everything changed. And the same is true with you and me.

We, too, have to learn to take our eyes off the storm and put them on the One who's ultimately in control of the storm and what it can do to us. We have to focus on Jesus.

It's the ultimate shift in perspective.

Extra Point:
Before Erika and I got the unfortunate call from the FBI about our lost investment, we'd already written out a check that would care for the needs of those twenty poor families in our community. But we hadn't told the families the money was coming to them, so we could still distroy the check and back out. All that the families knew was that someone wanted to bless them with something.

As a matter of fact, the pastor who was working with us told us that very few people knew about the money—so no one would judge us if we decided to not go through with it. The pastor had compassion with us, and he suggested that, at the very least, we give a lesser amount.

We were faced with a tough decision. What would you do if you were faced with the same predicament?

We prayed and fasted for several days, and we sensed God telling us to go ahead and give. He reminded us that it's His money; we just needed to be obedient in our stewardship of it.

So, we decided to give joyfully.

In a sense, we were shifting our focus from the storm to God—and trusting Him for our future. We still don't know how He would reward our obedience—in this life or the next. But we trusted Him, and we still do.

By giving the money we'd previously committed, we were able to buy a car for a family, pay several families' mortgages for a year, and provide tools for a man who was able to use them to make a living for his family. We were also able to buy Christmas presents and food gift cards for a number of families.

Of course, we had another decision to make, as well. We believed that part of trusting God was letting go of our dream house in North Carolina. We figured if God really wanted us to have it, He would've kept us in a position to buy it.

Besides, we'd just been reminded that the family in the house is a lot more important than the house itself.

So, we stayed in New Jersey.

In hindsight, we now know that New Jersey was exactly where God wanted us. Before we left Medford in 2014, we connected with a new church family and arranged two large Christian outreach concert events in the Marlton and Medford areas. God worked powerfully in people's lives through the events—and not just those who attended it. He worked in the lives of those who planned it and volunteered at it, as well.

All in all, Erika and I learned that if you're going to win in spite of whatever you're going through, you have to learn to shift your perspective from the problem to the other blessings in your life.

From the storm to God.

It was an expensive lesson, but we learned it well.

My wedding day, June 28, 1997

CHAPTER FOUR

Keeping the Main Thing the Main Thing

[Priorities]

"There are more important things in life
than winning or losing a game."

— LIONEL MESSI —

"I play to represent God, something more
important than baseball."

— ALBERT PUJOLS —

By October of 1998, three NFL teams had given me the chance to play for them, and all three had cut me. The first two times I was cut, it wasn't so bad. I knew going into the Carolina Panther's training camp in 1997, and the Atlanta Falcon's training camp in 1998, that I had very little chance of making their teams. They both already had All-Pro kickers in place.

But it was a much different experience getting cut by the Washington Redskins. The Redskins had promoted me to their starting kicker spot, and I had an incredible opportunity to get my NFL career rolling. But my debut game with the Redskins was so bad that they cut me less than forty-eight hours after the game. It was the lowest point of my career, up to that time.

Little did I know things would get even worse before I finally made it in the NFL.

Less than four months after getting cut by the Redskins, the Philadelphia Eagles gave me new life when they signed me to a one-year contract. They were willing to take a chance on me, but they first wanted me to play that spring in NFL Europe, a developmental league for guys who are trying to make it to the NFL.

I would play for ten weeks in Europe and then come back just in time for the Eagle's 1999 summer training camp. That's when I'd have another chance—probably my last— to make it in the NFL.

After going through a one-month training camp in Orlando, my NFL Europe team set off for Berlin, Germany, where I spent the next ten weeks—most of it away from Erika. I was the primary kicker for a start-up franchise that year, the Berlin Thunder.

The Marriott Hotel in the borough of Köpenick, Germany became my new home away from home, and each day, the team made a forty-minute drive from the hotel to our practice facility in the heart of Berlin.

The NFL Europe was made up of six teams that year, and our ten-game schedule consisted of home and away games with all the teams. That meant we visited each of the team's cities: Frankfurt (the Galaxy) and Düsseldorf (the Rhein Fire) in Germany; Barcelona (the Dragons) in Spain; Amsterdam (the Admirals) in the Netherlands; and Glasgow (the Scottish Claymores) in Scotland.

One of the bright spots of my time with NFL Europe was getting to see so many parts of Europe and experiencing so many different cultures.

I also loved one of NFL Europe's rules that is different than what we have in American football. Field goals from fifty yards or more were worth four points, rather than the usual three. I loved that aspect of the European game! To this day, I wish the NFL would adopt that rule. It added a great layer of strategy to the game—much like the three-point shot in basketball.

One of the not-so-bright spots of NFL Europe was the pay. I made one hundred dollars per week during training camp and seven hundred dollars per week during the season. It was a far cry from what I'd eventually make, even as a rookie, for the Eagles.

I also didn't like being away from Erika all that time. She was working at Lucent Technologies back in Atlanta, helping support my NFL dream. She used her limited vacation time to visit me once in the middle of my time in Berlin. But that was all I got to see her until I got back home.

Despite my team's optimism coming out of training camp, we weren't very good. We lost our first four games of the season on our way to a 3-7 record. We were last in the league. Honestly, I doubt that we could've beaten most of the top twenty-five college football teams that year.

Other than losing most of our games, the season went fairly smooth for the first eight weeks. But on the eve of our next to last game, one ordinary meal ended my season. And, unbeknownst to me at the time, started a chain of events that would change my life.

It was Sunday morning, a game day. The Frankfurt Galaxy was in town to play us at Olympic Stadium, and there I was, lying on the training room table, nauseated with cramping in my abdomen unlike any pain

I'd ever felt before.

The pain started the night before at the hotel. At first,
I was just feeling bad. Then I began to feel worse and my body
began to shiver. Then the pain became unbearable.

I called one of the team trainers who came to my room and
said I might have the flu. He gave me some homeopathic pills to help,
but they just ended up in the toilet a few minutes later when I threw
them up. A little later, my kidneys began hurting so badly that I filled the
bathtub with warm water and slumped down into it, hoping to soothe
the pain. That didn't help, either.

The next day, the trainer took me to the stadium early to
get me started on some IVs to see if I'd be able to play. But instead
of getting better, the fever, the pain, the vomiting, and diarrhea
continued to worsen. Finally, the trainer decided I needed to go
to the hospital. So, just like they do in war, they picked me up
on a canvas gurney and put me into an ambulance—where I rode
to the hospital by myself. I guess the team thought they
had a game to prepare for.

The hospital was in East Berlin, where English was not
commonly spoken. So, right away, we had communication problems.
My high school German wasn't taking me very far. The doctors
and nurses could tell from my facial expressions and pointing that I was
having severe abdominal pains. And, of course, the constant vomiting
and diarrhea were good clues that something dreadful
was going on inside of me.

I was dehydrated from the amount of body fluids I'd lost,
and the IVs they gave me couldn't keep up with the amount of
fluid my body was expelling.

The doctors and I weren't able to communicate very well
until another patient from England saw what was going on and
intervened as my translator. He was a sight for sore eyes, but I think he
was pretty sore as well. It looked like he'd gotten in a bad fight and was
on the worst end of it.

He conversed with the doctor for a while, and then turned to me and said, "You have a bloody one hundred five degree temperature, mate."

My translator also told me that my blood pressure was all over the place, spiking and then dropping and then spiking again. The doctor soon admitted me into the hospital and began running a bunch of tests.

On Monday morning, he came into my room and told me in very broken English that he'd figured out what was wrong with me— Salmonella food poisoning. They quickly put me into quarantine.

I still wasn't feeling better. Even though nothing was entering my body besides the content of the IV bag, I had to go to the bathroom nearly twenty times that first full day in the hospital.

When I say I had to "go to the bathroom," that really isn't an accurate description. The bathroom in my room was a wheelchair with a bucket, and I was quarantined to the room.

I didn't sleep much the entire time I was sick—which made the time drag on even longer. I had a lot of spare time on my hands. All that was in my room was a bed and that wheelchair with the bucket.

No radio. No TV. Nothing to pass the time.

I didn't even have an option for music. I had brought a CD player with a converter to Germany, but the first time I'd plugged it in at the hotel, I fried it.

And that was before cell phones were prominent, so I had little access to a phone. The only time I was able to talk to Erika was when the nurses would bring a landline phone with a really long cord to my room.

There was one rectangular window in the room that looked out over a building. Believe me, it wasn't a scenic view. I can't remember how many times I counted the clay shingles on the roof of the building I could see from my window.

I wrote several love letters to Erika. Honestly, I didn't know
if I would ever see her again. I knew little about Salmonella food poisoning, but I knew how I felt.

"I'm dying," I wrote to her several times.

I really thought I was.

On Monday, someone from the Thunder's front office
stopped by for a short visit, and he dropped off some books to
help me pass the time.

Let me tell you something about books and me: We didn't
exactly have the closest of relationships. Like I said earlier, I
passionately hate books. When I had to read growing up, it was
only because I was forced to. I was one of those kids who would stomp
off when my parents made me go read for school. I obeyed, but only
because I didn't think I had another choice.

But by Tuesday, I was going stir crazy, so I reached over and grabbed
Daniel Silva's *Mark of the Assassin* from the short stack
of books beside my bed. It was a mystery-type book involving
the CIA and a commercial airliner that blew up while in flight.
I won't say I couldn't put the book down, because I was still
making more than fifteen trips to the wheelchair bucket in a day.
But I thoroughly enjoyed the book. I would lie there as I read,
picture the characters, and envision the scenes of the story playing out. I
saw them in my mind almost as vividly as I could see the
roofline outside my window.

I quickly read that book and the three remaining on the
nightstand beside my bed.

Reading wasn't the only thing I did more than usual during my stay
in the hospital. I also prayed. A lot. It's amazing how being "deathly" sick
and helpless in a foreign country, thousands of miles away from family,
will cause you to think more about God.

Lord, please get me home to my wife, I'd pray in my mind.
I don't care if I play another down of football. Just let me get home.

They weren't the deepest of prayers, but there was a re-prioritization taking place in my life. I was in Europe for only one reason: I had a dream of playing in the NFL. Erika was completely on board with me pursuing that dream. But in that moment, I didn't care if I ever played football again. All I wanted was to be back home with my wife.

On Wednesday, my sickness showed the first signs of diminishing and the trips to the bucket decreased.

On Thursday, I had my first "meal"—oatmeal baby food. That little jar of food tasted better than any filet mignon I'd ever eaten. (And that's saying a lot, because I love a well marinated, lean tenderloin. Makes my mouth water just thinking about it.)

I finally was strong enough to check out of the hospital on Sunday, and I flew out Monday morning to Frankfurt on the first leg of my trip home. At the Frankfurt airport, I met up with some of my teammates who were booked on the same flight. I walked up to them, and they didn't even recognize me until I started talking.

I had lost thirty pounds.

My teammates in the Frankfurt airport weren't the only ones who didn't recognize me when they first saw. When I arrived in the Atlanta airport, Erika walked right past me. You know that cliché re-union scene where the man and woman run into each other's arms—after being apart—and give each other a big kiss? That didn't happen. Erika walked right past me toward another person until I flagged her down. She couldn't believe how bad I looked.

I visited a doctor in Atlanta and he told me, "You need two weeks to just do nothing. Try to get some strength back. Your body needs time to recover. Just relax and don't work out."

We had almost a month until the Eagles' training camp started, so Erika and I drove up to Hubbard Lake in Michigan, which was a favorite getaway spot for her family. We decided to drive there and simply spend time with each other and follow the doctor's orders to relax and do nothing.

Erika is a reader—or at least she was before we started having kids. On the drive up, she started telling me about a series of books she'd been reading called *Left Behind*, the mega-bestseller novels by Tim LaHaye and Jerry B. Jenkins that deal with the end of the world from a Biblical perspective.

Before that time, Erika and I were believers in Christ, but we hadn't yet become followers.

If Erika had told me about that series before my East Berlin hospital stay, I wouldn't have even considered reading them. But because of the massive amount of reading I'd just done—and enjoyed—I became curious about the *Left Behind* books.

Erika had the books with her in the car, and since she was driving, I pulled out the first book and read the first ninety pages in what felt like a blink of the eye.

"This book is awesome!" I kept telling her.

I knew the book was fiction, but I became curious as to whether the Bible verses it referenced were real. I read some more of the books during our vacation and became even more curious to read the Bible. But neither of us had brought a Bible on the trip. (It wasn't really central to our lives at the time.)

As soon as we returned home from vacation, I took a Bible and began looking up the scriptures referenced in the *Left Behind* books.

Wow! I would think as I read the scriptures. *This is true!*

Then I wanted to take into account the full context of the passages I was reading, so I read entire chapters of the Bible at a time.

God's Word came alive to me like never before. I'd grown up attending church and listening to the pastor's sermons—and I worked on urban-renewal projects as a teenager—but I came to realize that I was missing out on the most important thing: a true relationship with Jesus.

The more I read the Bible, the more I felt like I was coming to know God, and the more I felt like I was growing in relationship with Him.

After checking out the passages referenced in the books, I decided to read the whole New Testament. I immediately read through the gospels.

I've heard people say that the more they get into the Bible, the more it gets into them. Well, that really happened with me during that season of my life. The more I read, the closer I got to God. And the closer I got to God, the more my priorities began to change. The shift that began in my hospital room in East Berlin continued in the weeks leading up to the Eagles' training camp.

That season of my life taught me that to *win in spite of* the pain in your life, you have to figure out what's really most important and prioritize accordingly. Prior to my bout with Salmonella, I would've said Erika was more important than football. But I hadn't really prioritized my actions in a way that affirmed her as being more important. When I thought I was going to die, there was no question that she was more important than football.

That's one of the upsides to suffering. It helps us reconnect with the true priorities of our life.

In just a few months, my priorities reversed from Football-Family-Faith to Faith-Family-Football.

It's a shift that's defined my life ever since.

First Things First

Looking back, I see how God used my Salmonella experience to reorient my life around a new set of priorities—before my NFL career even started.

In fact, once I got my priorities straight, that's when my career started.

Even as those priorities were solidifying, I entered the Eagles' training camp, earning a job as their Kick-Off Specialist and Long Field Goal Kicker for the first year. I became their starting kicker the next year. Once again, I had the chance to learn, for a year, under a veteran kicker, Norm Johnson, who was their starter for a number of years.

As it turned out, football in Philadelphia became the focus of much of my life for the next twelve years. But it would never again be my top priority. And that has made all the difference for my family and me.

> *"I try to spend as much time as possible with God and my family. That's more important than anything I'm doing in baseball."*
>
> — ALBERT PUJOLS —

You see I work in a profession where the divorce rate has been estimated by *The New York Times* to be as high as eighty percent. That's a lot higher than the national average for divorce, which has hovered around fifty percent for a while. There are few things I dread more than being a part of that statistic.

For all it's perks, being a professional athlete can come at a price when you're trying to make God and family your highest priorities. The natural flow of things can easily destroy your relationship with God—and your marriage.

For one thing, NFL players have to spend a lot of time away from their families. We're away weeks at a time for training camp, and then we have to travel a good bit during the season. We travel from city to city, where we stay in a lot of hotels. And when we become free agents or get traded, we find ourselves having to quickly relocate to another part of the country, often months before our families can join us.

In the midst of all this separation, both players and their wives get lonely for companionship. To use a baseball metaphor, that's strike one against faith and family.

Secondly, pro athletes have lots of adoring fans. Our job requires us to be in good shape, and to some degree or another, we have fame and money, too. Some fans are drawn to that, and they have their own game to play. They want to see whom they can score with. I'll spare you the R-rated version, but I've watched many of my teammates get taken down by adoring fans over the years. That's strike two.

Thirdly, the whole pro football culture promotes big egos and little self-control. It's a self-centered environment that calls out to the flesh. I had to battle it my whole NFL career. When the media spotlight is on you, and millions of people are watching you, it's hard to not let it go to your head. Imagine doing your job in front of millions of people, knowing that they actually care how well you perform. It's a little scary, for sure, but it's also very affirming to your ego—especially when you perform well. That's strike three.

You can see why so many players strike out with their faith. There are so many opportunities for them to feed their flesh. And many do. It's also why so many NFL marriages strike out.

For Erika and me, it's all come down to priorities. From the very beginning, I figured out what's more important between winning on the field and winning at home. Many pro football players have put their performance as a husband and father as a much lower priority than their performance on the field. I didn't want that.

But I've had to work very hard to keep my priorities straight. I've had to be very careful at times. And I've had to be very proactive.

Erika and I aren't close because it's easy. We're close because we work on it. All the time. We've always made sure to make time for us. For many years, we kept a date night sacred each week so we could connect and make sure we focused on each other—even if our night out consisted of dinner and a walk around Target to get toiletries.

Are there times when I'm completely selfish? Oh, yeah. I'm human, and I'm not always easy to live with. I know what the Bible says, and I stand on God's Word, trying to be the husband God has called me to be. But I fall short—a lot more than I want to.

Despite my weaknesses, Erika knows I have a heart for her, and I'm in our marriage for the long haul. She also knows I'll never quit working on being a better husband. So when I mess up, I admit my failure, apologize, and keep working on it.

Many marriages fail because both spouses are too worried about how the other makes them feel. They're asking what their spouses do to complete them, and if their spouses make them feel happy and significant. Those are the wrong questions to be asking! They're a set up for marriage failure because no one can do for their spouse what only God can do.

Ephesians gives us the model for what being a husband, or wife, should look like. And it's not an easy model to live up to.

"Wives, submit yourselves to your own husbands as you do to the Lord. For the husband is the head of the wife as Christ is the head of the church, his body, of which he is the Savior. Now as the church submits to Christ, so also wives should submit to their husbands in everything. Husbands, love your wives, just as Christ loved the church and gave himself up for her.... In this same way, husbands ought to love their wives as their own bodies. He who loves his wife loves himself. After all, no one ever hated their own body, but they feed and care for their body, just as Christ does the church" (Ephesians 5:22-32).

So, we husbands are suppose to love our wives like Christ loves the church? Are you kidding me? Jesus gave everything for the church. His example is radical. Extreme.

Perfect.

Men, that's our model, as we love our wives. It's also a pretty good model for how we should love our children. It's the model I'm trying to live up to.

Am I the world's best dad? Not even close. Do I push my kids too hard some times? Probably so. I'm tough on them because I don't want them to settle for anything less than God's best. But at the same time, my kids know I love them and want their best.

It's why I tuck them in at night (it's the best time to get their attention), pray with them (I make sure they hear me pray out loud), sing over them (even with my bad voice!), and encourage them (Erika and I are their biggest cheerleaders).

I'll be straight up, the temptations of the NFL life are very hard to resist. At times, the money has gotten too much of my focus, the accolades have gotten to my head, and the lure of adoring fans has tempted me. But for the most part, I've tried hard to stay away from people and places that would encourage me to act on those desires.

> *"Your biggest opponent isn't the other guy.*
> *It's human nature."*
> — BOBBY KNIGHT —

I have priorities that are much more important than the temporary high of those things.

When I get tempted, I think about how important God is, how precious Erika is, and how much of a blessing my kids are. That's why I say no to the other stuff. They're like garbage in comparison. And they're not my priorities.

So far in this chapter, I've told you my story. But what is your story? What are your priorities?

It's one thing to say that God and your family are your priorities, but it's another thing to live like it. If you're putting anything else ahead of the commitments you've made to them, stop it. No matter what it takes.

Actions Speak Louder

I've heard this phrase many times: "The main thing is to keep the main thing the main thing." It's another way of saying that we should put first things first—and keep them first. The Bible is clear about what the main thing is.

Once a teacher of the Old Testament law asked Jesus: "Of all the commandments, which is the most important?" In a sense, he was asking Jesus what the main thing is.

Jesus replied that the most important one is this, *"Love the Lord your God with all your heart and with all your soul and with all your mind and with all your strength. The second is this: Love your neighbor as yourself. There is no greater commandment than these"* (Mark 12:28-31).

Can't get any clearer than that. Loving God is first. Then loving your neighbor is a close second. Together, that's the main thing.

In His Sermon on the Mount, Jesus said something similar. He preached that we should stop putting so much of our focus on money and material things because God already knows we need them, and He's committed to taking care of them.

Jesus said, *"But seek first [God's] kingdom and his righteousness, and all these things will be given to you as well"* (Matthew 6:33).

It's not that money and material things aren't important in our lives—just try to live without them! But we're to seek God first—and then those things will come. If we're trusting in God, He'll take care of the rest.

Are you keeping God as the main thing?

> "Our greatest fear should not be
> of failure but of succeeding at things
> in life that don't really matter."
> — FRANCIS CHAN —

Be honest. How often do you say that God is most important, and then you let other things influence your decisions on how you spend your money, occupy your time, and live your life? Seriously, your actions speak louder than your words!

Bottom line: Your priorities aren't what you say they are. They're what your life shows they are.

God's Wink

It's very hard, sometimes, to put God first and trust Him to take care of all our needs. Especially when God doesn't work in our time-frame, we take our needs into our own hands. That's when we allow our priorities to get whacked out.

A few years after I started playing for the Eagles, God reaffirmed to me that He could indeed be trusted to take care of my family's needs. His affirmation came when I messed up on our tithe.

To begin with, I tithe differently than most people. When I was still playing, I knew what I was going to make each year—it was all contracted—and I gave my complete tithe at the end of the year because that's when I made most of my money for the year. Most players receive their money over a seventeen-week pay schedule during the season. I got paid every Tuesday and then got the pay stub that showed me the money on Wednesday. It was always nice to see that pay stub!

I was never sure if I should be tithing on my net or my gross income. I asked my pastor one time, and he told me in a joking manner, "If you tithe on the net, you'll get a net blessing. But if you tithe on the gross, you'll get a gross blessing!"

I always think of that and laugh whenever I hear people debate the subject.

In 2003, I sat down at the end of the year to write the check for our annual tithe. It was always a little painful to write a check that big. But it was even more painful a short time later when I got my giving statement for the year from my church. It said I had written a check for the same amount in the spring. In other words, I had double-tithed!

I had totally forgotten that I'd decided to be proactive that year, and I gave early.

At first, it was hard to think that I'd given away so much money, but then I realized I wasn't even missing it!

I thought, *If tithing should bring me joy—as the Bible says—than shouldn't a double tithe bring me double joy?*

Then something really cool happened.

Three weeks after I signed and released the second check, I received a phone call from my marketing agent. A major corporation was offering me the biggest endorsement deal I'd ever received at that time. And in the first year alone, I was paid exactly—to the penny—the same amount of my gross tithe for that year.

Whoa, that's amazing! I thought. *Are you trying to tell me something, God?*

Maybe some people would think it was a coincidence, but I saw it as a wink from God. It was like God was showing me that regardless of how much I gave; I wasn't going to out-give Him. His actions spoke even louder than His Word. He gave me confirmation of Matthew 6:33—that if I sought Him first, He would take care of all our needs. I haven't forgotten that lesson to this day.

Now, I know that God doesn't always reward our faithfulness in such big and obvious ways. Sometimes He rewards us in this life, and sometimes we have to have faith that He's storing up treasure for us in Heaven. He's not a name-it-claim-it God who will give us everything we want, when we want, the way we want—if we'll just claim it and believe it's ours.

I've gone from giving reluctantly to giving joyfully. I remember having a conversation about tithing not long after that with my friend and teammate, Brian Dawkins, on a plane trip home from a game. Dawkins was a nine-time All Pro safety for the Eagles during my time with the team, and he, too, was named to the NFL All Decade Team for the 2000s. Brian is also a fellow Christ-follower.

Brian told me, "I love giving to the church because of all the great things it does in people's lives."

I couldn't agree more.

If you haven't already, it's time you put first things first—not just with your words, but also with your actions. And with your money.

If you do, the rest will fall into place.

Gameday for the Berlin Thunder in the NFL Europe [Spring 1999]

Some of the wonderful staff that took care of me at the East Berlin Hospital [1999]

The hospital room in which I was quarentined [1999]

CHAPTER FIVE

Fuel the Fire

[Passion]

"If you aren't going all the way, why go at all?"
– JOE NAMATH –

I played for the Philadelphia Eagles for twelve years, and I have to tell you, I loved the Philadelphia fans. In fact, when my time was done with the Eagles, I bought billboard space in a high-traffic area off of Interstate 95 to thank Philly fans for their years of enthusiastic support on and off the field.

I felt like Eagle's fans had invited me into their family home and had treated me like one of their own.

I've traveled to every NFL city during my career, so I've experienced fans just about everywhere. And I have to say there's something extra special about Philly fans. I know, I'm a little biased, but Eagles fans are one of the most passionate groups of people you'll find anywhere. Seriously!

Eagles football is like a religion in Eastern Pennsylvania and South Jersey. When I played there, Lincoln Financial Stadium was like a cathedral, where the religious faithful would worship on Sundays. And I guess Andy Reid was the priest, and beer and pretzels were the communion elements.

The New York Giants, Dallas Cowboys, and Washington Redskins were part of the evil force that we were called to fight. And booing the refs and shouting obscenities were definitely Eagles' fans' hymns of choice. (They sang those hymns to me a time or two!)

Eagles' fans are passionate when they win and equally passionate when they lose. When I hit a big field goal, I was the hero of their faith. But when I missed a big kick, I was the sacrificial goat.

On game day, most Eagles fans dress in green, wear player jerseys, paint their faces, and some even paint their bodies. And those are the ones at home watching the game on TV!

Some fans are so passionate about Eagles' football that their emotional tone for their week is determined by whether or not the Eagles win.

Admittedly, some Philly fans are a little whacky, but here's one thing I love about them: They don't give up on their team.

The Eagles gave their fans quite a bit to cheer about when I played for them, but that hasn't always been the case. There was a bad stretch of seasons before I played there. And our fans were just as committed to the team in the losing years as they were in the winning years. Yes, they complained! And yes, they gave owners, coaches, and players a lot of grief! But they never gave up on their team.

Whether the Eagles win or lose, Philly fans maintain their passion.

What Is Passion?

I think it's easier to recognize passion when you see it than it is to define what it is. If I asked you to tell me what passion is, you'd probably stumble through your answer. But if I asked you to name a passionate person, you could probably do so with no problem.

The original meaning of the word *passion* is "to suffer." In the Christian faith, Passion Week is the week of Jesus' suffering. And Mel Gibson's movie, *The Passion of the Christ*, was about Jesus' suffering—which it showed in a *very* graphic and brutal way.

Today, our idea of passion has more to do with a strong conviction or a commitment to something you believe in. The reason you know it when you see it is because conviction and commitment show up in the ways we act. They influence what we do and how we do it.

Passion is the emotional fuel that keeps us going. It's like wind in our sails that carries us forward. It's like gasoline that keeps our car engine running.

It's fuel for our life.

*"Each of us has a fire in our hearts
for something. It's our goal in life
to find it and keep it."*

— MARY LOU RETTON

You can probably think of several people you know who
are very passionate about something. Maybe they're passionate
about life, in general. If I asked you to name NFL players who
are passionate, you might think of Tim Tebow or Reggie White.

But when I think of NFL players who show a lot of passion,
the first person I think of is my former teammate Brian Dawkins.

Brian used to say, "I'm gonna act a fool." And he played with
a lot of emotion.

Early in his career, he earned the nickname Wolverine. Heck,
he even had a nameplate on his locker that said "Weapon X."
So, instead of running out of the tunnel into the stadium before
the game like everyone else, he came scurrying out on all four
of his hands and feet like a Wolverine. Then when he got to the beginning of the player's line where the cheerleaders were standing, he'd jump
to his feet, flex his ripped biceps, and shout out a battle cry as he ran
through the lineup of players on both sides.

On the field, Brian played with a lot of passion, as well. He
threw himself around with reckless abandon to shake blocks and make
tackles. Pound for pound, he was the hardest-hitting safety
I ever played with—or against. Our opponent's players cringed at
the thought of getting hit by him.

What I loved about Brian is that he exhibited the same
passion in the rest of his life as he did when he was in a game. He was
passionate about his family, his church, and most of all, God.

Do you know anyone who attacks every aspect of his or her life with
that kind of passion?

*"Men are born to be passionate warriors.
We were put on this earth to fight battles
that matter. But the battles we choose
aren't always the right ones, so we have
to let God channel our passion to fight
the battles He wants us to fight."*
— JOHN HARBAUGH —

I played with a lot of other passionate people in my career, and I've learned that passion isn't always expressed with the kind of emotion that Brian had. Some people have quieter, more reserved personalities, so their passion is not quite as loud.

One example was my head coach in Philadelphia, Andy Reid. Andy showed his passion calmly and quietly, but we knew it was there. We saw it in his work ethic. We saw it in his concern for his players. We saw it in how he did things with excellence. And we saw it in his commitment to the team and to winning.

My second NFL coach was Jim Harbaugh. Jim and Andy couldn't have been more different. Where Andy stayed calm, Jim got fired up. Where Andy led by example, Jim led by inspiration. Was Jim more passionate than Andy? I don't think so. He seemed like it at the time, but I knew the deep level of Andy's commitment. Was Jim more committed to winning than Andy? Again, I don't think so. Both were among the best coaches in the league. Both were winners.

For two years, I also had the chance to play in Philadelphia with outspoken wide receiver, Terrell Owen. Terrell was another one of those guys who played with outward intensity and emotion. You usually didn't have to wonder what Terrell was thinking. If his actions didn't tell you, his mouth probably would.

Terrell was definitely known around the league for being fiery and outspoken, but he was also known for how committed he was to his workouts and training schedule. He kept his body in great shape and, like Dawkins, pushed himself at a high level on and off the field.

But NFL players and coaches aren't the only ones who live with passion. Most everyone is passionate about something. Some of us are passionate about interests or hobbies like a college or professional sports team, a certain type of music, coffee, skiing, NASCAR, fishing, cooking, traveling, shopping, etc. The list could go on and on.

Of course, most of us are also passionate about more important things. Maybe you're passionate about your family, your church, your community, your local school system, or some part of government.

Maybe you're passionate about feeding the hungry, fighting human trafficking, protecting the environment, or caring for orphans.

I'm passionate about some of those things, too, but my greatest passion is for God. I'm passionate about worshipping Him, serving Him, and telling others about Him.

Take a moment and think about what things you're passionate about. What are you doing with those passions? If God gave them to you, don't you think He did so for a good reason?

Passion is important because it helps define our priorities, and it also helps us to persevere when things get hard. That's why passion is a crucial element for *winning in spite of* the hardships and failures in our lives. It fuels us.

Your passion will keep you from giving up when things get hard. It will keep you in the game after you fail.

Your passion for the things that are important will make you persevere for them when nothing else will.

I've always been passionate about my dream of playing in the NFL, and more than once that passion has kept me in the game when it seemed like I might be done. You've already heard about how I stuck with my dream (with help from Erika) after being cut by the first three teams that gave me a shot. But that wasn't the only time my passion fueled me to hang on.

Life After Philly

When my playing days were done in Philadelphia after the 2010 season, my family and I went through a hard time of transition.

I felt like I was a boxer who had just been knocked to the ground by a series of punches. The first punch was when we lost our life's savings in the Triton fiasco. The second was when doctors found a cancerous tumor in my daughter's ovary. And the third was when I wasn't able to reach a contract agreement with the Eagles.
At that point, I was a kicker without a team.

As the offseason wore on, it became more and more clear that the player's union and the league weren't going to reach an agreement by the start of the 2011 training camp. We were headed for a lockout.

At that point, teams weren't thinking much about shoring up their rosters for the coming season like they normally would. That meant I would have to wait longer to get an offer. But after the way I'd bungled our last playoff game against the Packers, would I even get one?

I was very motivated in the off-season leading up to the 2011 season. I desperately wanted to get back on the field for three reasons. One, I needed to provide for my family by earning back some of the savings I had lost with Triton. Two, I wanted to get back out there as soon as possible and perform at a high level so I could get rid of the bitter taste of my last playoff game with the Eagles. And three, I knew in my heart I wasn't done. I knew I could still kick at a Pro-Bowl level.

The passion generated by those three motivational forces pushed me to train harder than I'd ever trained before.

With a lockout looming, I joined several of my former Philadelphia teammates to work out with Steve Saunders, who is a well-known NFL strength and conditioning guru. We pushed each other every day. If someone did twenty pull-ups, I would go all out to do twenty-one. And then one of the other guys would push as hard as he could to one-up me. I could keep up with them in the weight room, but it was a different story when we did our running conditioning. They left me in the dust!

But, hey, I'd like to see them try to outkick me!

My training partners joked that I had a linebacker stuck inside my kicker's body. I was never satisfied. Always pushing harder. I was in the best shape of my career.

The time for training camp to start came and went with no agreement between the Player's Association and the NFL. After four months of negotiations, we were all beginning to wonder if there was even going to be a 2011 season.

Finally, on July 25, the lockout came to an end. It was time to get back to work.

Except I didn't have a team to go to work for!

With the lockout behind them, teams could begin signing free agents. And fortunately, some good offers started coming my direction. I narrowed my choice down to the Washington Redskins and San Francisco 49ers. Each had its strengths and weaknesses, but I went with the 49ers. The tiebreaker was that I really wanted to play for Jim Harbaugh. Why? For one thing, I loved his passion.

I went into the 2011 season feeling as good as ever—physically, mentally, and emotionally. I knew that the passion that pushed me through an uncertain offseason was going to be a game-changer for me. Literally.

*"You're either in or you're out.
There's no such thing as life in-between."*
— PAT RILEY —

My first preseason game as a 49er was against the New Orleans Saints. I had one fifty-nine yard kick, and I made it. That got me off on the right foot. (Well, in my case, it got me off on the left foot—but you know what I mean.)

That season turned out to be my best ever. I ended up making a personal single-season record seven kicks of more than fifty yards, and I made it into the *Guinness Book of World Records* by kicking an NFL season record forty-four field goals. I also surpassed Jerry Rice's record for most points in a season by a 49er.

But none of that would've happened if my passion for my family and for the game hadn't pushed me through a difficult, uncertain off-season to be ready for anything in the 2011 season.

The Passion of Jesus

Jesus is our greatest example of passion. He was passionate about doing the will of His Father, and He pursued what the Father called Him to with everything He had. He was also passionate about us, and He went to extremes to restore a relationship with us. He died a brutal death for us!

So, why aren't we more passionate about Jesus? If it weren't for Him, we'd all be living in spiritual darkness—and on our way to hell.

In chapter four, we already saw that God has called us to love Him with all our heart, mind, soul, and strength. With everything we've got! And that same passage said we should also love our neighbors with the same kind of passion with which we love ourselves. Those two verses are connected. Loving God passionately overflows in loving people the same way.

God wants our passion, and He'll call us out if we have a passionless faith. When He was judging the churches in the Book of Revelation, He called out the Laodiceans for their lack of passion.

"I know your deeds, that you are neither cold nor hot.
I wish you were one or the other! So, because you are lukewarm—
neither hot nor cold—I am about to spit you out of my mouth"
(Revelation 3:15-16).

Wow, that's some strong language! God *spits out* those who are halfhearted and lukewarm about their faith! I didn't make that up. God said it.

I once heard well-known pastor, author, speaker and friend, Francis Chan, compare this passage to drinking coffee. When you drink coffee, do you prefer it to be hot or lukewarm? Think about it. If you took a drink of lukewarm coffee, what would you do? I'm guessing you'd spit it out. I would!

Now, some people like their coffee ice cold. I'm not personally a big fan of iced coffee, but I have friends who are. And when they get a glass of iced coffee, they don't want it lukewarm, either. They want it ice cold. If they took a swig of what they thought was iced coffee and it was lukewarm, they'd spit it out, too.

My point is simple: Coffee is nasty when served at room temperature. And apparently, so is our faith.

Let me say it as plainly as I know how: Your lukewarm faith is nasty to God. That's why He spits it out!

God is looking for a radical few who will live with a white-hot passion for Him.

"For the eyes of the LORD range throughout the earth
to strengthen those whose hearts are **fully committed** *to him"*
(2 Chronicles 16:9, emphasis added).

While I lived in San Francisco, I met some people who showed me

what it looks like to be on fire for God. They showed me that when you passionately love God—so much so that you're willing to sacrifice and suffer for Him—you'd also passionately love people.
The two go hand in hand.

Passion for People

As hard as it was to leave Philly, I knew that the move to San Francisco would give my family and me a fresh start. And I was determined that I wanted to go to new levels on and off the field. I wanted to kick so well that I'd erase the memory of that horrible playoff game against the Packers. And I wanted to make sure my growing relationship with God was permeating every part of my life. I wanted my love for Him to show at all times.

As soon as I got to San Francisco, I connected with the team Chaplain to let him know he could count on me for help. I told him I wanted to be a guy that players knew they could come to because my actions matched what I professed to believe as a Christ-follower.

Looking back on my time in San Francisco, I had some incredible highs and lows as a kicker. But as a Christ-follower, I lived my life more consistently for what I believed than I ever had before. Heck, my teammate, Randy Moss, started calling me "The Rev."

I started by bringing guys together before we went out on the field to start the game. I would try to come up with a theme that would be appropriate based on the team we were playing or an issue that was affecting the team.

I challenged the guys to not be lukewarm about their faith. And I challenged their hypocrisy. It was too common for guys to profess their faith in Christ with their mouths but not back it up with their actions.

I would often tell them: "You can't make God your genie in a bottle on Sundays and then go hit the strip joints on Mondays. It doesn't work like that, guys!"

I connected with players all season long and encouraged them to live lives that reflected their profession of faith.

In October of the 2011 season, the 49ers traveled to Philadelphia to play the Eagles. It was my first time to go back there in another uniform.

The Niners chaplain asked me if I could get someone in Philly to come speak to our team for the pre-game chapel. So, I asked my friend and former pastor, Jon Wegner, to speak. He shared a basic, but powerful, message from Matthew 7 about the wise man that built his house on the rock and the foolish man who built his house on the sand. He then asked us where we've built the foundation of our lives—on the rock or on the sand. At the end, he asked us to bow our heads and raise our hands if we'd like to build our lives on the Rock that would not fail us when the hurricane winds of life blew.

Six of my teammates raised their hands and prayed with him that evening to place their faith in Jesus and build their lives on His Word. Several were well-known starters.

Just a few months into my first season with the Niners, I already felt like God was using me to have a spiritual impact on my team. Meanwhile, I was also helping my team win games.

About midway through the season, my friend and ex-teammate, Tony Stewart, asked me to have dinner with him and a couple of his friends at Akikos, his favorite sushi restaurant in San Francisco. Little did I know that time would bring to the surface my passion for loving the poor and marginalized.

One of Tony's friends who came to dinner that evening was Christian Huang, the executive director of San Francisco City Impact—a ministry that existed to serve the inner-city poor and provide opportunities for them to find a new way of life.

Tony's other friend who joined us for dinner was a well-known author and speaker, Francis Chan.

It was a powerful conversation with three people who would become great friends, mentors, and ministry partners—while eating the best sushi I've ever eaten in my life.

I sat there soaking in their wisdom like a kid sitting cross-legged at the feet of his grandfather. I was in awe as they shared stories of what God was doing in the lives of some of the most needy people in San Francisco through City Impact.

Their spiritual passion for the least and lost burned so hot that I could see it and feel it.

I walked away from that meeting knowing that I had to be a part of it. (That's the thing I've learned about passion. It drives our actions.)

As I left the restaurant that evening, I thought, *God, You've stirred in me a passion for something that I know You're passionate about. Now, show me how to take action!*

Not long after that, I met again with Francis at the Blue Bottle coffee shop in San Francisco. This time, I had the best coffee I'd ever had in my life, and Blue Bottle became one of my favorite hangouts when I lived in San Francisco.

Francis reminded me of the importance of using my God-given gifts and platform to serve those who didn't have the same opportunities I had. He shared with me how God had led him and his family to leave the awesome church he was pastoring to work with "the least of these" in San Francisco. He took time to show me in the Bible how God's heart breaks for the poor, oppressed, and hurting.

Over the next few months, my passion to serve the poor continued to burn hotter. I didn't just want to serve the materially poor, but also the poor in spirit. I began to realize that some of the wealthy people I knew were materially rich, yes, but they lived in spiritual poverty. I gained a passion to minister to the needs of both the materially and spiritually poor that were all around me.

I met another very passionate person during that time that God also used to stoke the flame of my spiritual fire. Her name is Heidi Baker, and she runs Iris Ministries in Mozambique, Africa. Her ministry to poor children and families can be summed up in two words: radical love.

I'd heard about Heidi several times, from several different people, in several different places. If Francis stoked the flame of my passion, she flat out blew it up as she told me about all the miracles that God had done through her ministry to the poor and homeless in Mozambique.

> *"I am building a fire, and every day I train, I add more fuel. At just the right moment, I light the match."*
>
> — MIA HAMM —

Francis's passion is to live life with a crazy love—which, by the way, is also the name of his best-selling book. And Heidi's passion is to live life with a radical love—which is also the name of her book.

Because of my time with these two heroes of faith, I came away more crazy and radical about showing love than I'd ever been before.

Contagious Passion

I learned something about passion as I spent time with Christian, Francis, Heidi, and others like them.

Passion is contagious.

When we're around people who live their lives with full-tilt conviction and commitment, they stir our own conviction and commitment. Those who express it in emotional ways often stir us emotionally. They inspire us! And those who express it more quietly often elevate our own commitment and conviction in a quieter way, too—over time through their example. They show us the substance of their actions.

Both are important to our lives.

As you know by now, I got to play for John Harbaugh when he was my Position Coach in Philadelphia. And in San Francisco, I got to play for his brother, Jim. Both of them are very passionate people who inspired me in different ways.

Because I played longer and worked more closely with John, I got to know him a lot better than Jim. I mainly interacted with Jim in passing moments on the road, during team meals, and, of course, at practice and in games. But I interacted with John both on and off the field for hours at a time over eight years.

Both were passionate in their praise and in their rebuke.

One game, John tore into me on the sidelines because I wasn't precise enough with the placement of an onside kick. I kicked it three yards too far.

Just three yards!

When I returned to the sideline, he jumped all over me like I had done something unforgivable. He got hot, and I responded in kind. I'll leave most of it to your imagination, but it ended with me telling him he could go find another kicker if he didn't like my kickoffs.

Of course, I was the one who was out of line. I didn't like him calling me out for something that seemed so small to me. But when I cooled down, I knew he was right. It wasn't the level of excellence that either of us wanted from me.

Yeah, I did a lot of apologizing for that one!

But what impressed me is that the next time I saw John off the field, he asked me how I was doing. He wanted to know how Erika and the kids were. More than anything, I think he wanted me to know that he had left his heated words on the field.

He was just as concerned for me as a person as he was for me as his player.

I got a unique perspective by playing for both of the Harbaughs. I realized that they, too, had "caught" their passion from someone else—their father, Jack. They both used family phrases and mottos with their teams that they'd picked up from Jack throughout their growing-up years.

Here's my favorite: "Attack each day with an enthusiasm unknown to mankind!"

It's a phrase that they repeat often to their own kids and players. But more importantly, they live it out.

See, the Harbaughs aren't just passionate about football. They're passionate about life. And they make others around them more passionate about life, too.

That's how I want to live.

How about you?

Extra Point:

Fire is used throughout the Bible as a symbol for the presence of God (see *Deuteronomy 4:12 and Hebrews 12:29*). In Exodus, the Holy Spirit led the way for the Israelites as a pillar of fire as they escaped their Egyptian captors (see *Exodus 13:21*). And in Acts, when the Holy Spirit came upon the apostles, they saw visible fire (see *Acts 2:3*).

I find it interesting that when we see people who are passionate about God, we talk about how they're "on fire for God." Maybe that's because God's presence is with them.

Unfortunately, many who call themselves Christians have no fire to their faith. It's passionless! That's what happens when our idea of being a Christian is church attendance and our idea of church is an irrelevant religious institution.

A passionate faith is a whole lot more than church attendance. It's about making God the centerpiece of your life and being willing to sacrifice everything for Him.

I want my life to burn with passion for God. But I'll be honest, life has had a way of pouring water on my faith. At times, my flame has been reduced to a flicker, or even a burning ember.

But just as physical fire can be fueled and refueled, so can spiritual fire.

Worship fuels it. Prayer fuels it. Reading God's Word fuels it. And so does being around people who have a passionate faith. It's like they pour gasoline on our faith. That's what Christian Huang, Francis Chan, Heidi Baker, and John Harbaugh have done for me.

Likewise, we also have people in our lives who drain our passion for God. Some are constantly critical. Some constantly talk about others behind their backs. Some encourage us to do or say things that violate our values and priorities. And as they do these things, they pour water on the flames of our faith.

Think about your life. Who are the people who fuel your passion for God and for the other things in your life that are important? Who are the people who drain your passion?

Maybe you need to pull away from some of the drainers in your life and spend more time with the gainers—those who fuel your faith. Maybe you need more of God's Word, prayer, and worship in your life to fuel your spiritual fire.

Whatever you do, don't settle for a lukewarm faith.

Family Christmas cards during my time with the Niners [2012]
photos by bill frakes

Christian Huang, Francis Chan, and Tony Stewart
at Akikos Restuarant in San Fransisco [2011]

Heidi Baker of
Iris Ministries
and me [2011]

SECOND HALF
Playing to Win

If you're going to play to win, you have to start with a winning mindset. That's what the First Half was about. But ultimately playing to win happens on the different playing fields of our life.

Winning takes a team, and it takes a lot of preparation, but it also takes a willingness to go out on the field and give it everything you've got. Every time your number is called.

It's one thing to think and talk like a winner. It's another thing to follow through with the actions of a winner. You don't win in sports—or in life—by sitting on the sidelines. You win by getting in the game and living out the truth that you say you believe.

CHAPTER SIX

Get in the Game

[Participation]

"I want to be in the lineup every day. Playing anywhere is better than playing the bench."

— ALBERT PUJOLS —

This is a play-by-play dramatization of an actual event. Seriously, this really happened!

ANNOUNCER: The Philadelphia Eagles trail the Tampa Bay Buccaneers, 13-5, with just twenty-three seconds remaining in the first half. It's third and ten, and the Eagles are at the Bucs' eleven yard line. Philadelphia has no time outs remaining, so they either need to score a touchdown here, throw an incomplete pass, or get out of bounds to stop the clock so the Field-Goal Unit can have time to get onto the field.

COMMENTATOR: Yeah, the worst-case scenario here is for the Eagles to complete a pass and then not get it into the end zone or out of bounds to stop the clock.

ANNOUNCER: Quarterback Doug Peterson is under the center for the Eagles with Fullback Kevin Turner lined up in the backfield. Peterson takes the snap and drops back. He's looking into the end zone to find a receiver. No one open there. He looks to his right and checks it off to Turner coming out of the backfield. Turner heads for the sidelines, but Bucs' Cornerback, Donnie Abraham, is closing quickly, and…oh, Abraham stops Turner for just a two-yard gain.

COMMENTATOR: And more importantly, Abraham made the tackle before Turner could get out of bounds. That's exactly what the Eagles didn't want! Now, they can't stop the clock! It's still ticking!

ANNOUNCER: That makes it fourth and eight for the Eagles at the Bucs' nine yard line, and now Andy Reid has just nineteen seconds to get his Field Goal Team out onto the field to take a shot at what looks like a twenty-six yard field goal.

The Eagles' players are moving fast to get set up for the field goal before time expires. But the clock is running down!

It looks like the Eagles are about set up, and Doug Peterson is in place for the hold with his back to the Eagles' sideline. But I don't see Kicker, Norm Johnson, anywhere.

Where is he? The seconds continue to tick off the clock!
The Eagles are almost out of time!

COMMENTATOR: I've never seen anything like this before!
The Field-Goal Unit is on the field, but there's no kicker!

ANNOUNCER: Wait! There he is! Apparently, he's been warming up
at the kicking net. Okay, Norm Johnson is now running out on the
field—snapping up his chinstrap. But I don't think he has enough
time to get there for the kick before the half expires!

COMMENTATOR: Wow! Johnson's teammates on the sidelines
just parted like the Red Sea to let him come through from the back
of the sideline area.

ANNOUNCER: This is going to be close! The clock is down
to five, four, … and Peterson goes ahead and calls for the
snap before time expires! Johnson has to wheel around him
to make the kick, but he can't get set. He just swings his foot at the
ball to get the kick up in the air. And it's an ugly, off-kilter, wobbly
kick.

And the kick…is…no good! It goes wide to the left!
And the Eagles blow an easy scoring opportunity!

COMMENTATOR: That's unbelievable! The Field Goal
Unit did what it was supposed to do. They were on the field
and set up, but the kicker was nowhere to be found! What
was Johnson thinking?

ANNOUNCER: Apparently, he wasn't thinking. His head wasn't
in the game, and now, the Philadelphia crowd is really giving
it to Andy Reid and the Eagles players as they run off the field to the
locker room.

COMMENTATOR: Wow, that's a lot of booing!

ANNOUNCER: You have to wonder who dropped the ball on
that one. Was it Special Teams Coach, John Harbaugh, or was
it Norm Johnson? I'm sure Andy Reid will be asking some
questions to find out at halftime.

COMMENTATOR: Well, there's no reason for your kicker to not be ready to go when his team needs him. There's just no excuse for any player to be on the sidelines when he should be in the game!

True Story

Like I said, the story you just read is true! This was my own play-by-play account of it, but the facts are accurate. In my first year as a pro, my friend and mentor, Norm Johnson, was a "no show" for his own field goal!

I was standing on the Eagle's sideline when it happened. I was the Kick Off Specialist and Long Field Goal Kicker at the time, and Norm kicked all our shorter field goals. And this was about as short of a kick as you get.

When Norm was missing in action, my heart started thumping. A litany of thoughts ran through my head, and I about ran out there and kicked it myself!

Where is Norm? I thought. *He was just standing here with the Field Goal Unit! Should I run in and kick it for him? Will I get in trouble if I do? Oh, I can't go in! Doug isn't set up to hold for a left-footed kicker! There's no way he can get reset for me in time!*

Norm, where are you!?

John Harbaugh told me later that he was concerned about losing his job when Norm was a no-show for that kick. John had to go back and show the videotape to Andy to prove that he did, in fact, have his Field Goal Team—including Norm—ready to go. Norm had just wandered back to the kicking net to continue warming up his leg.

To his credit, Norm didn't make any excuses for not being there when he was needed, but he told us he thought Doug Peterson was either going to throw for a touchdown or throw the ball away. Either way, he didn't think he was going to be up against a running clock for his kick. But as we'll see in chapter seven, you have to be prepared and ready for anything.

Of course, the Philadelphia media had a good time with this one. That week, the paper printed an editorial cartoon that gave their take on why Norm didn't show up for the kick.

According to the cartoon, Norm was at the concession stand getting a slice of pizza for Andy.

Now, I want you to know that Norm was only a no-show once in his career. He learned from his mistake—and so did I. I made sure I was always ready when the Field Goal Unit was called on. Never once did I come up MIA when it was time for me to kick.

Thanks, Norm, for teaching me that lesson!

Actually, I have Norm to thank for teaching me more than that lesson. He was a good kicker, and I was fortunate to play with him. He taught me a lot during our short time together with the Eagles.

But that wasn't Norm Johnson's best day.

Missing in Action

Looking back on it now, the whole thing is funny. But at the time, nobody on the Eagles' team was laughing. Our coaching staff didn't quickly forget about it.

Like the commentator in our opening dramatization said: "There's just no excuse for any player to be on the sidelines when he should be in the game!"

Maybe you're already tracking with me on this, but the same is true in life. You can't be a winner if you're sitting on the sidelines—especially if it's your turn to be on the field. You can only be a winner if you're in the game. Where the action is.

> *"Do you know what my favorite part of the game is? The opportunity to play."*
> — MIKE SINGLETARY

God inspires all of us to take a step of faith at different times in our life. But the sad truth is that most aren't willing to step out when He calls. Some are afraid. Some are apathetic. Some are distracted by other things. Some are too comfortable where they are in life. And some are so insensitive to God that they can't even hear Him calling.

But make no mistake; God has called you to get in the game. He's called you to live a faith story that only you can live. He's called you to participate in His game plan.

Let me put it bluntly: He's called you to get up off your butt and do something with the time, talent, and treasure He's given you.

"For we are God's workmanship, created in Christ Jesus to do good works, which God prepared in advance for us to do" *(Ephesians 2:10).*

God apparently wants you to have splinters in your hands from working, not splinters in your butt from sitting on the bench.

God has *prepared in advance* good works for you to do. He's thought about it, and He's given you an important role to play in the greatest contest ever—the one where eternal life is the prize for all who play to win.

God never meant for His salvation to just be fire insurance so you can get to Heaven and avoid Hell. When you become a child of God, He invites you to follow Him and be a part of His work in people's lives all over the world.

He invites you to join the team and participate in the game.

All through the Bible, God called on different people, and He greatly used those who said, "I'm in." But what could He do through the life of someone who wouldn't follow Him and participate in His plan? Not much.

When God called Noah to build an ark that would take his family more than a century to build, Noah said, "I'm in." And then he set out to grow some trees so he'd have the wood to build it.

When God called Abraham to leave behind his family and home and go to an unknown place that God would later show him, Abraham said, "I'm in." And then he stepped out in faith—leaving his family and home behind.

When Moses cried out to God for Him to deliver the Israelites out of slavery from the Egyptians, God told Moses to step up and lead the Israelites himself. Moses mumbled about not being able to communicate very well, but, ultimately, he said, "I'm in." And then he became the leader of the Jewish nation.

When God needed someone to repair the broken walls around Jerusalem, Nehemiah said, "I'm your guy." And then he launched a monumental effort to repair the walls and restore a fortified Jerusalem.

When God called Isaiah to be His prophet, Isaiah said, "Here am I. Send me." And Isaiah became one of the greatest prophets in the Old Testament.

When Jesus called out to Andrew, Peter, James, and John as they were fishing and told them to follow Him, they replied, "We're in." And then they left their fathers, their careers, and everything that was familiar to follow Him.

But not everyone said, "I'm in."

Remember the rich, young man in Mark Chapter ten who Jesus asked to sell his possessions and come follow Him? The young man turned away because his wealth was more important to him than following Jesus.

We don't know what this man's name was. But if he had participated in Jesus' game plan, maybe there would have been a fifth gospel named after him. Had he said, "I'm in," we might be reading the "Gospel according to Reggie" or "The Gospel According to Ted," or whatever his name was.

But we'll never know, because his money was more important than aligning himself with Jesus' game plan.

What's keeping you from saying, "I'm in"? Like Norm Johnson, who didn't show for his kick, do other things distract you? Are you too much into "doing your own thing" to do God's thing? Are you too apathetic? Are you too afraid?

Whatever has kept you on the sideline, it's time you said, "I'm in." It's time for you to get in the game and participate in whatever way God leads.

> *"There is a point in every contest when sitting on the sidelines is not an option."*
>
> – DEAN SMITH –

Being Where the Action Is

I've often thought about the difference between the second-string players who have to sit on the bench most of the game and the first-string players who are in the game, where the action is. When you're in the game, you get to make a difference. You get the rush of adrenaline that comes with knowing your teammates are counting on you.

When you're a second-string player, you miss the pure joy and adrenaline rush of being in on the action. It really sucks when you have to watch the game from the bench, rather than playing it on the field.

Fortunately, in life, we don't have to be second-string players who sit on the bench most of the time. We get to be in the game, and in on the action.

If we choose to.

In Chapter five, I mentioned that I became friends with people like Christian Huang, Francis Chan, and Heidi Baker during my time in San Francisco. They introduced me to God's heart for the "least of these" and called me to participate in the ministry to the poor.

They showed me that when you answer God's call and step out in faith to go where the poor live, God shows up in powerful ways.

I thought, *Heck yeah! I want to be where God is working!*

They told me powerful stories about the incredible miracles God did as they gave their lives to sacrificially serve the poor. Here's just one of the many.

A few years ago, San Francisco City Impact decided to put on their first-ever City Impact Conference, which trained ordinary people how to minister to the poor and homeless. I didn't go to the conference that year, but I went to one a few years later. It was amazing!

The day before the first conference, they realized attendance was going to be a lot higher than they thought.

City Impact's chef came to Christian and said, "How are we going to feed all these people? We don't have enough food!"

They didn't have enough money to go get more food, so they decided to cut the portions in half.

And then they prayed. Hard.

Later that day, a local Trader Joe's called and asked if they needed any food. The manager said their power had gone out and their refrigeration units weren't working. They needed to unload a lot of food before it went bad.

City Impact suddenly had plenty of food to feed the conference attendees.

Now, was that just a coincidence?

The story doesn't end there. The next year, in the days leading up to the second conference, it happened again. They once again grossly underestimated the attendance at the conference.

And just like he did one year before, the chef went to Christian and said,

"What are we going to do? We don't have enough food…again!"

Christian replied in an ironic tone, "I don't know. It's not like God has never multiplied food before!"

They laughed and then they prayed.

Later that day, Trader Joe's called again. This time their freezer had gone out, and they had a lot of meat that they needed to unload before it thawed.

"Will you take this off our hands?" the manager asked.

Once again, conference attendees had plenty to eat.

Still think it was a coincidence? Maybe once, but twice? Really!?

As I've sacrificed things in my life to serve the least and lost, I've found that God shows up in amazing ways when we pray and sacrificially do the work He's called us to do.

Let me put it a different way: When we pray and participate, God participates, too. And as we all know, He's a game-changer!

God has made you to do good works, to get in the game and make a difference in the lives of other people. The greatest way you can win, in spite of the pain and hardship in your own life, is to help others get through their pain and hardship, too.

In fact, God will use your pain—if you let Him—to help you better empathize and participate in the lives and pain of others.

So, I ask you one more time: Are you going to stand on the sidelines or get in the game? Are you going to stay where it's nice and comfortable, or are you going to get on the playing field where the action is—where God shows up?

You can't be a winner if you aren't in the game.

Overtime win in the playoffs against the Packers [2004]

CHAPTER SEVEN

Ready for Anything

[Preparation]

"If you fail to prepare, you're prepared to fail."
– MARK SPITZ –

When you play on a Special Teams Unit in the NFL, you learn a few things, right away. For one thing, you learn that you have to be ready to go into the game at any time. For another, you learn that you have to be ready to respond to just about any game-time situation.

Here's an example. In the 2000 season, my Eagles team was behind 23-13 with 3:42 remaining in the fourth quarter against the Pittsburgh Steelers in the old Three Rivers Stadium. Our quarterback, Donovan McNabb, took just one minute and thirteen seconds off the clock to drive our team deep into Steelers territory, where he hit running back, Brian Mitchell, for a thirteen-yard TD pass, with 2:29 remaining. That cut our deficit to three points (23-20).

On the ensuing kickoff, Coach Andy Reid called on me to kick an onside kick, which is one of the most precise things I ever had to do as a kicker. The Kickoff Team practiced it over and over each week so we'd have our timing down if called on to do an onside kick in a game. We were ready.

I kicked the ball exactly where I was supposed to, and one of our "sure hands" guys recovered it exactly like he was supposed to. Well, almost exactly like he was supposed to. He recovered it nine-and-three-quarters yards from where the kick took place. By NFL rule, it has to go ten yards before our guy can recover it.

At the time, it was a penalty that required us to back up five yards and re-kick. So, we got lined up again and did the same thing from five yards deeper in our own territory.

Once again, I placed the ball exactly where I was supposed to, and this time, the ball took a crazy bounce and shot down the forty yard line where our safety, Tim Hauck, dove on it.

Our offense now had the ball back with about two minutes remaining. That was plenty of time for Donovan to get us at least into field goal position so I'd have a shot at tying the game.

And he and the offense did just that. They drove the ball down field and set me up for a forty-two-yard field goal.

Problem was, they didn't leave us much time to get our Field Goal Unit out on the field. With just seventeen seconds left, no time outs, and the clock running, we had to get out on the field, set up, and get the snap off before time expired. It was a race against the clock.

As Chris Berman would say, "Tick, tick, tick, tick, tick, tick, tick."

I didn't have enough time to mark off my steps before the kick. I had to eyeball it and go.

Our long snapper, Michael Bartrum, got the okay from our holder, Koy Detmer, and he snapped the ball with two seconds on the clock. My foot hit the ball as the clock hit zero, and I drilled it through the uprights to tie the score at 23-23.

We were headed to overtime!

We got the ball first in the extra period and Donovan did the same thing that he'd done at the end of regulation. He drove the offense down the field to move us into field-goal position. But this time, the Field Goal Unit had plenty of time to get on the field and in position for the kick.

It was another forty-two yard attempt, but this one was much easier. I could actually mark off my steps and go through my usual pre-kick preparations.

I hit the field goal, and we won the game 26-23.

By the way, just a week earlier, I had hit a game-winner on the road against the Dallas Cowboys to give us a 16-13 victory. Those back-to-back winning kicks pretty much solidified my job with the Eagles. I would be their starting kicker until 2011, and I would end up scoring more points than any Eagle player, ever.

Now, if you look back through NFL game records, you'll find something that tells you we won the game against the Steelers, 23-20, on November 12, 2000.

But there's something the records won't tell you.

See, we really didn't win the game *that* day. We won it on countless days before when we practiced onside kicks. And on all the days when we worked on getting our Field Goal Unit on the field quickly for a "hurry up" kick.

I guess what I'm saying is that we really won that game in practice. Because hours and hours of practice had prepared us for the scenarios we faced in Pittsburg that day.

No Shortcuts

Each year, NFL teams hold a mini-camp right after the NFL draft, in May. It's a long weekend where they bring together the existing players with new draft picks and off-season acquisitions, and they begin taking a look at the team they've put together. That's also when they pass out the playbook for the year.

My first-ever mini-camp was in May 2000, and I spent a good bit of that weekend with John Harbaugh. The first time we got the Field Goal Unit together to practice against the Field Goal Block Unit that weekend, John had us do something that I thought was totally bizarre at the time.

He had us practice "hurry-up" field goals. Andy Reid called in an offensive play to Donovan McNabb, and the Offense ran the play in a scenario where the clock was winding down, and we didn't have any timeouts. The coaches made sure we knew that the clock would stop with an incomplete pass, or if our player caught a pass and ran out of bounds. But they also made sure we knew that the clock would *not* stop if the play ended in a sack or a receiver was not able to get out of bounds. In that case, the Field Goal Team would be called out for a hurry-up field goal attempt.

Our coaches wanted the Field Goal Team to be able to get on the field and the ball snapped in seventeen seconds or less. That was our target.

Seventeen seconds!

I was thinking, *C'mon Andy and John! This is the way you're going to start mini-camp? Really? We'll never be in this kind of situation, and you're starting our year with this? I'm no expert here, but shouldn't we be practicing normal game-day situations, first?*

In a sense, I was right. I only had to do two hurry-up field goals in my whole career. But our coaches were communicating something with their actions that they would then preach with their words all that season, and every season thereafter.

"Be ready for anything."

Now, you know why we were able to execute our hurry-up kick in that game against Pittsburgh. We had already done it dozens of times in practice. Andy and John had us ready for anything.

Not every team was prepared like we were. Just a week or two later, I saw on ESPN's Sports Center that another team had more than twenty seconds to get their Field Goal Unit on the field to kick a "hurry-up" field goal, and they didn't even get the snap off before time ran out. That's when I realized just how well Andy and John had prepared us for anything on game day.

It's partly what makes them such great coaches to this day.

"I didn't believe in team motivation. I believe in getting a team prepared so it knows it will have the necessary confidence when it steps on the field and be prepared to play the game."

— TOM LANDRY —

There's just no way around it. Teams don't win in the NFL because of talent alone. They win because they're talented *and prepared.*

Teams prepare six days a week for one game on Sunday or Monday (or now on Thursday).

Game-day preparation is not just physical. It actually starts with the mental aspect of the game. Teams spend a lot more time studying "film" and talking about their game plan than they do actually practicing it on the field.

Coaches spend sleepless nights preparing for their opponents. Then they put together schemes that exploit the other team's weaknesses and shut down their strengths.

They also get their players ready for the opposing players they'll match up against. Players have to know their opponent's tendencies so well that the game is "slowed downed" for them—so they can react to what they see in the game without even thinking about it.

Even the most talented players and best teams can't perform well if they're not mentally prepared for each game. (That's why we spent the first half of this book getting ourselves mentally prepared to *win in spite of* the hardships in our life.)

Likewise, teams spend a lot more time on the practice field than they do playing the game. Practice starts in mini-camp, goes through two-a-days in training camp, then through the pre-season, all the way through the season itself and into the post-season.

It's a grueling amount of practice. But it's critical to team success.

Repetition in practice allows the team to develop the individual skills and team timing to make them like a well-oiled machine on game day. It allows them to be ready for anything.

Ten-Thousand Hours

In his book *Outliers*, author Malcolm Gladwell says it takes about ten thousand hours of practice for a person to master any field of performance. Gladwell studied (and cited other studies about) the lives of extremely successful people to find out how they achieved success.

Gladwell cited a study from the early nineteen-nineties where a team of psychologists in Germany studied the practice habits of violin students from their childhood through adulthood. They found that by the age of twenty, the elite performers had already averaged more than ten thousand hours of practice each, while the less able performers had only four thousand hours of practice. In other words, the elite performers had more than double the amount of practice hours of the less able performers.

The study concluded that talent didn't actually factor into the performance capabilities of those they studied. Instead, the psychologists found a direct statistical relationship between the hours the violinists practiced and how good they were. That's it.

No shortcuts.

Just practice.

The same was true of the others that Gladwell studied who'd made it big—including entrepreneurs like Bill Gates and musicians like "The Beatles." All of them had put in at least ten thousand hours of practice time before they made it big with their talent. (By the way, to help you understand what ten thousand hours of practice look like, just think of yourself working at something forty hours per week for five years. That's roughly ten thousand hours.)

Gladwell noticed something else in his research: The elite don't just work harder than everybody else. At some point, they fall in love with the actual act of the practice, to the point where they want to do little else.

> "It's not the will to win that matters—
> everyone has that. It's the will to
> prepare to win that matters."
> PAUL "BEAR" BRYANT

I guess there are two ways you could apply Gladwell's conclusions to your life. Either you could choose a field of performance and practice ten thousand hours, or you could find something that you're already good at, because you've accumulated a lot of those practice hours, and then work to become even better at it.

But here's the thing. It's important that you choose to get good at something you're passionate about because ten thousand hours is a lot of time to practice anything.

It seems much shorter when you enjoy what you're doing. And as you probably already know from experience, it seems a lot longer if you don't enjoy what you're doing.

Passion and preparation really do go hand in hand.

So, what tasks do you perform so well that people ask: "How did you do that?" "What thing do you love doing so much that it hardly feels like work when you do it?"

In my case, I began kicking a soccer ball when I was six years old, so it came natural for me to transition into kicking a football in high school.

Playing American football was an unlikely proposition in my mind. I was one-hundred-and-forty pounds of blue twisted steel my junior year in high school. I was solid, but not quite big enough to be a linebacker.

I was going to be a soccer player, and my goal was to become a college standout at the University of Kentucky, which was near my Lexington home. But one day, all that changed when I was playing a pick-up football game with a bunch of my friends at my high school's football-soccer field. On a whim, I told one of my friends to put the football down so I could try a field goal. It was forty-five yards away from the goal post, but I took a shot at it anyhow. I booted the ball as hard as I could, using the soccer form that was familiar to me, and to our shock, I made the kick! It not only went far enough, but it was also accurate enough!

One of the guys playing with us was the son of one of our football coaches, and he let his dad know about my impromptu kick that day. A few weeks later, his dad approached me and asked if I wanted to be the Kicker for the football team. Problem was, football season was the same time as soccer season. No way I was trading soccer for football.

Actually, I wanted to play both!

Before long, I was trying to convince my parents and my soccer coach to allow me to play both soccer *and* football. My parents agreed as long as I kept up a 3.0 grade-point average. And my soccer coach was very supportive as well.

As it turned out, the hours I had put into soccer actually helped me gain the speed, agility, balance, and leg strength I needed for kicking in football. I was good at both soccer and football, but there were a lot of players as good as me in soccer. And there weren't many really good field-goal kickers my age.

Obviously, football ended up winning over soccer.

I practiced and practiced my placekicking skills in high school and college. Then I practiced some more as I played for NFL Europe.

And then I practiced some more as I played with Carolina, Atlanta, and Washington in the NFL. During that time, I went to Florida for three months and practiced my kicking technique with Doug Blevins.

And I worked my way into becoming the full-time Kicker with the Eagles as I practiced even more.

So, it will come as no surprise that I had practiced pretty close to ten thousand hours by the time I became a full-time NFL starter.

Now, here's what's incredible about my professional football journey. I thought that my time with Carolina, Atlanta, and Washington were all times of failure. But now I see it from a different perspective. Those experiences actually added to my ten thousand hours of mastery as a professional placekicker!

And better yet, some of the NFL's greatest kickers ever were my teachers!

In Carolina, I learned from veteran, All-Pro kicker John Kasey that I needed to develop a more consistent technique. He taught me how to keep my body more square to my target as I kicked through the ball. And he showed me how to distribute my body weight as I kicked.

One of the most helpful things John taught me was a simple drill called a One-Step Kick, which really helped me maintain my proper kicking technique. I ended up using it as a warm-up drill for my entire career, and it was one of the biggest reasons I was able to maintain proper form.

John also taught me to kick the ball with just eighty-five percent of my total power so I could maintain accuracy and replicate the kick over and over. The key to being consistently accurate is to create a form that you can precisely repeat every time. And John was the first person to tell me that I must make at least ninety percent of my field-goal attempts as an NFL kicker.

John really gave me the foundation for my kicking that I was able to build on the rest of my career.

In Atlanta, veteran All-Pro Kicker Morten Andersen answered literally hundreds of questions that I pelted him with over our five months together. Morten gave me the nickname "Q," which stood for "Question Boy." He was nice enough to answer all of my questions, and he shared with me the training regimens and body-maintenance tips that allowed him to play in the league for more than two decades. I think he added years to my career.

Morten was already a legend by the time I worked with him. And I'll be honest; I was in awe of him! I had looked up to Morten for years since he was also a strong, left-legged kicker like me.

I thought to myself, *I couldn't buy this type of knowledge!* So, I was determined to ask questions until he stopped answering them. And to my surprise, he never did!

In my time with Doug Blevins, I learned how to compete with other highly talented kickers. Doug critiqued my every kick to point out when I wasn't being consistent in my form—regardless if I made the kick or not. With Doug, it was all about the kind of consistency that would give me confidence to hit the kick every time I stepped on the field.

In my time with the Redskins, I learned not to get so amped up for a kick. (Remember the horrible game I had with Washington against the Seattle Seahawks?) I learned to channel that adrenaline in other ways so I wouldn't "over kick" the ball every time. I learned when it was okay to "let it go" and when I needed to back down and "smooth it."

And in my first year with the Eagles, veteran kicker Norm Johnson taught me a lot about what it takes to be a kicker in the NFL by taking care of the little things.

I rode into practice with Norm every day of my first season with the Eagles, and he showed me how to address the daily grind of the regular season. On our rides into work, we talked about everything from finances and taxes to what was the optimal amount of kicks I should make during my pregame routine. Norm was with me nearly every day that season, and I learned a ton from him by just watching the way he handled different situations.

And I also need to mention punter Sean Landetta, another Eagles' Special Teams players that taught me a lot in my early years with the Eagles. Sean played twenty-five years in professional football—in both the NFL and USFL—and he showed me how to capitalize on my football platform to take advantage of the many opportunities it provided. When I was with Sean, I felt like I was in a college course in marketing. Heck, maybe even a graduate-level course!

Sean was a consummate professional who performed well

on the field for years, and then used his football platform to participate in corporate and charity events in the community. He showed me how to use my NFL platform to serve people in my community.

And then there's John Harbaugh, the guy I played for in Philadelphia for twelve years. As you've already seen, he demanded excellence from me and got me ready for any game-day situation. But he taught me so much more than the game of football. On the field, he taught me how to carry myself as a professional and as a team player. And off the field, he modeled how to be a great husband, father, friend, mentor, and passionate Christ-follower.

To this day, I am amazed at the people God has put in my life who took the time to prepare me as a kicker, professional, businessman, philanthropist, family man, and Christ-follower.

They're all a part of my personnel team life (which I'll share more about in the next chapter). And their instructions had been a critical part of my training as I put in the practice hours to be a top-level NFL kicker.

Spiritual Training

So, what does all of this have to do with this book? Sure, practice is important for athletes, but what does it have to do with life?

A lot.

What happens when no one is watching us greatly affects what happens when they are.

I've shown you how this principle is true in football: Teams practice for days with no cameras around (except for our own field cameras that help us study what we're doing right and wrong) so they can play at a very high level for three hours on game day when millions of people are watching.

But it's also true in many areas of your life. For instance, the time you invest in spiritual disciplines, like prayer and studying God's Word (when no one's watching), greatly affects your thoughts, actions, and reactions when temptation or trials come.

When times are good, we must strengthen and prepare our hearts and minds for the times when they aren't so good. That's why I believe that preparation is one of the keys to winning in spite of the trials in your life. If you're preparing when times are good, you're ready to face whatever comes with the hard times.

One of the core pieces of our preparation in football is our playbook. Each team member has to know the plays—and what his particular role is in each play. In life, God's Word is a lot like the team playbook. It tells us what God wants from us and shows us how to live in a way that pleases God and impacts other people's lives.

That's why I've used the Bible as the guide for the principles in this book. It's our Life Playbook.

As I mentioned in chapter one, the apostle Paul was likely an athlete, and he often compared our spiritual life with athletics in his letters to different people and churches. Once, when he was writing to his "son in the faith," Timothy, he exhorted him to train spiritually just like he would physically train if he were an athlete.

"Train yourself to be godly. For physical training is of some value, but godliness has value for all things, holding promise for both the present life and the life to come" (1 Timothy 4:7b-8).

Did you catch that? Physical training is good for this life, but spiritual training has value for both this life and for all of eternity.

In a letter he wrote to the Corinthian church, Paul used another sports metaphor to liken spiritual training to physical training.

"Do you not know that in a race all runners run, but only one gets the prize? Run in such a way as to get the prize. Everyone who competes in the games goes into strict training. They do it to get a crown that will not last, but we do it to get a crown that will last forever. Therefore, I do not run like someone running aimlessly; I do not fight like a boxer beating the air. No, I strike a blow to my body and make it my slave so that after

I have preached to others, I myself will not be disqualified for the prize"
(1 Corinthians 9:24-27).

Now *that's* some hardcore training! Are you running in such a way as to win the prize? Have you gone into strict training? Are you beating your body and making it obedient to God's Word and His calling on your life? Or are you going through life lazy and without a sense of purpose.

If you haven't gone into spiritual training, it's time to get up off your butt and start!

At the end of every off-season, I went into to strict training to get ready for the upcoming season. I strained every muscle as I lifted in the weight room. I pushed as hard as I could as I ran wind sprints. I kicked over and over until my leg felt like it was going to fall off. I did all that to win that elusive prize known as the Super Bowl ring.

But more importantly, I'm in spiritual training to win a different prize that lasts forever. I'm training in such a way that, after writing and speaking these things, I won't be disqualified for the prize.

How about you? Are you training each day with an intensity that God deserves? And more to the point of this book, are you training in a way that will leave you ready for whatever life brings your way?

I realize you can't totally prepare for every possible trial you might face, but you can prepare the state of your heart, mind, and spirit for times when life gets hard.

Tools for Training

As I mentioned earlier, the Word of God is critical to our training.

"All Scripture is God-breathed and is useful for teaching, rebuking, correcting and training in righteousness, so that the servant of God may be thoroughly equipped for every good work" (2 Timothy 3:16-17).

God's Word trains us in righteousness so that we'll be equipped to do good works. It renews our minds and prepares us to face both the easy and hard times.

Prayer is also a critical part of our training regimen. When you draw near to God in prayer, He draws near to you. And when He draws near to you, He changes your focus and thinking. He brings peace where there's no stillness in your spirit, hope where there's no visible prospect for a desired outcome, wisdom where there's no understanding, and direction where there's only confusion.

When we pray and study the Bible, God renews our mind, refocuses our priorities, and restores our hope so that we can handle whatever comes our way.

Our time alone with God is critical preparation for our lives. It's the core of our spiritual training.

But we also must train with the community of believers, as well. If the Bible is our playbook, then the church is our team.

In football, we gather with our teammates most of the week to prepare for Sunday. But in life, we gather with our team on Sunday to prepare for most of the week.

It seems to me that we need to gather with our teammates more than once a week!

Prayer, Bible study, and gathering with other Christ-followers are all critical parts of our training routine.

Are they each a part of yours?

Extra Point:
My record-tying sixty-three yard field goal in 2012 didn't just happen by luck. It happened because our Field Goal Unit performed nearly flawlessly on that kick.

We had practiced long kicks like that over and over in preparation for that day.

And I had made that kick so many times in practice—with and without the full Field Goal Unit—that I knew I could make it in the game. Especially on a fair-weather day, when the wind was not much of a factor.

But here's what I want you to notice. I made that kick in my thirteenth year as a full-time kicker. By that time, I was seasoned. By that time, I probably had ten thousand hours in just practicing long kicks of more than fifty yards. I knew all the mistakes that kickers make when they're attempting a kick from that far out. I knew them because I had made them many times myself.

I made that kick because the Field Goal Team and I were prepared, and we responded to the challenge.

If the Long Snapper would have been off with his snap, it may have thrown off our timing. If the Holder didn't get the ball down and positioned, I probably wouldn't have connected with the ball cleanly. And if the Front Line hadn't brought down the Packer players, who were jumping high for the block, I probably wouldn't be talking about this kick right now.

But on that day, everyone did their job, and we made history—at least for another year until the record was broken.

If you're early in your attempt to do anything well—parent your children, start a business, take on a new role at church, develop a new skill, teach a class, or anything else—you will fail along the way. But keep working at it. You will get better. You may not be ready to set records right now, but who knows, thirteen years from now you might be.

If you've been doing something for a long time, maybe it's time to challenge yourself. Maybe you need to push the boundaries of what you've accomplished in your area of expertise in the past. Or maybe it's time to start something new.

I don't believe that God wants us to rest on the laurels of our past successes.

When I retired from kicking, I believed God was calling me into a new season of service to Him and others. I believed He was calling me to speak in corporate and ministry settings. And I believed He was calling me to write this book.

But I had very little formal training in speaking or writing. So, what did I do?

I started preparing.

First, I built a team of personnel to help me. I got a booking agent to help me with the business and marketing side of my speaking, and then I got a speaking and content-development coach who helped me organize my thoughts and raise the impact of my speaking to a higher level.

I knew I didn't just want to say words when I spoke. I wanted to impact people's lives, and he helped me do that. Like John Kasey and Morten Andersen, he took the natural talent I had and helped me fine-tune my technique and elevate my skill so that I could "play" at a higher level when I stepped out on a stage.

At the same time, I went after it from every other angle—just like I had done in the late nineties with my football dream. I got a literary agent and some help with media. And I asked a lot of questions of my teammates who were already speaking and writing. Just like I did with Morten. (Thankfully, nobody has started calling me "Q" yet.)

Being successful at anything requires passion for what you're doing, a team of people (or personnel) who can help you with your goals, perseverance to not give up when you fail, and a whole lot of preparation so you can perform at a high level when it's your turn.

CHAPTER EIGHT

Life Is a Team Sport

[Personnel]

"The strength of a team is each individual member.
The strength of each member is the team."

PHIL JACKSON

My first-ever football coach was at Tates Creek High School
in Lexington, Kentucky. His name was Roy Walton, and he was a gray-
haired, leathery, tough, no-nonsense, old school philosopher who had the
nickname "The Silver Fox."

Like many other high school coaches, Roy didn't coach for
the paycheck. He coached because he loved football.

And he loved kids.

And like many coaches of his day, he did and said things that probably wouldn't fly today. He would often grab us by the facemask to get
our attention, and once he had it, he would sometime say things that
would've made people cringe by today's standards.
Yes, there were usually a few expletives involved.

But we always knew Roy was looking out for our best.

He would often give his players a ride to and from practices
and games because their parents either couldn't or weren't willing to. On
the field, he was a tough disciplinarian. But off the field, he was
a more wise and gentle mentor, counselor, and father figure.

Roy deeply impacted my life and the lives of many other young
men over the years before he died in 2010. His funeral was packed with
hundreds of former students who wanted to say goodbye to their coach,
teacher, mentor, and friend—the Silver Fox.

Roy wasn't one who cared what other people thought. He
reminded me of the character Curly, played by Jack Palance,
in the movie, *City Slickers*. Curly handed out his life philosophy
that was learned through a lifetime of experiences.

"Life is about one thing," Curly said as he held up one boney finger.
"This."

"Your finger?" comes the reply from the middle-aged man, Mitch,
who's gleaning his wisdom.

"One thing. Just one thing. You stick to that, and the rest
don't mean sh**."

That's what Roy was like. He had a rough and rugged way about him as he taught his students and players lessons about life. He handed out his life wisdom in his own crude and crusty way.

Although he said a lot over the years that has stayed with me, he said something at my senior year football banquet that I think about the most. Roy was about to retire, so he was more reflective at this banquet than usual.

"I had someone recently tell me that I'm a self-made man," he said in his Curly-like way. "But there ain't no such thing as a self-made person. You can't do nothin' on your own. Everyone needs other people."

I couldn't agree more. I learned from Roy that all of life is a team sport. You need others, and they need you. And that lesson has been confirmed through experience over and over throughout my life.

I am the person I am today because of people like Roy Walton who have taught me, inspired me, challenged me, encouraged me, shown me, confronted me, and believed in me.

So are you.

I pray for my kids to have even a few high-impact coaches and mentors like Roy Walton.

Team, Team, and Team

It's a common saying that the three most important things in real estate are location, location, and location. Well, I have something similar to say about football. The three most important things are team, team, and team.

I think the same is true of life.

Having committed and caring personnel in your life is one of the most crucial things for *winning in spite of* the hardships you must face. I know that sometimes people are the main source of our problems.

But on the flip side, we wouldn't make it through
life without the encouragement and support of other people.

I agree with Coach Walton: Life really is a team sport.

In football, I was a part of a team, and each of us on the team
had our role to play. The Kick Off Unit and the Field Goal Unit
were dependent on the Offensive Unit, Defensive Unit, and
other Special Teams Units to do their job. Every unit depended
on the others.

And within the Kick Off and Field Goal Units, I had ten
other guys on the field with me that I depended on. And they
depended on me.

When the Field Goal Unit took the field, I depended on the Long
Snapper to get off a good snap. I depended on the Holder to handle
the snap cleanly and get it down quickly—so it wouldn't throw off my
timing. And I depended on nine different guys—
everyone but the holder and me—to block on-coming defenders
so they wouldn't be able to block the kick.

And they depended on me to kick the ball through the uprights and
put points on the board.

There are some sports that award individuals. But in football,
we all share most of the awards. If one of us wins the game, we
all do. If one of us loses the game, we all do. If one of us get's a
Super Bowl ring, we all do.

When John Harbaugh was my Position Coach in Philadelphia, he
would always talk to us about the importance of operating like
a team. And he would insist that everyone had to do their best
because everyone else was counting on them.

His team philosophy goes like this: Each person has to give one
hundred percent every time he steps onto the field because every
other player on the team needs his best effort. What an
individual player does, doesn't just affect him. It affects the coaches,
the fifty-two other players on the team, and a whole lot of other

people who work for the organization.

That's why it would always hurt so badly when I would miss an important kick. I knew my coaches and teammates were counting on me.

As a kicker, I got all the credit when our field goal team made the kick—even though I couldn't have done my job if they didn't do theirs. And I got all the blame if we missed a kick—even though sometimes it wasn't my entire fault.

I always understood that making a field goal, or extra point, was a team effort. And each of us was counting on the others.

That's why John doesn't put up with it when some of his players aren't giving an all-in, all-out effort.

"Where else would you rather be than right here, right now?" he sometimes asks his players. "Would you rather be at home in bed right now? Would you rather have another job? Would you rather be on another team?

"You've been dreaming about playing in the NFL your whole life. Now, this is where you are. God put you here. But what are you doing with your opportunity? Are you squandering it because you're being selfish and lazy? If you're going to play for this team, selfishness and laziness won't be tolerated. Because you're not just letting yourself down. You're also letting down everyone else in this locker room."

He then points to the doorway. "Gentlemen, the door is right over there. If you're not going to give it a one hundred percent effort for your team, then you need to walk out that door right now. But if you don't choose to walk out that door, than I want your best effort every time you step on the field.

"You don't have to be on this team. But if you choose to, you're choosing to be a part of something that's bigger than yourself. So, you have to act like it."

> *"The way a team plays as a whole determines its success. You may have the greatest bunch of individual stars in the world, but if they don't play together, the club won't be worth a dime."*
> — BABE RUTH —

The same could be said about our lives. You're a part of someone else's team, and they depend on you. When you're selfish or lazy, you let them down.

If you're a parent, your children are counting on you. If you're a spouse, your husband or wife is counting on you. If you're an employee, your employers and co-workers are counting on you. If you're a leader, your followers are counting on you. If you're a Christ-follower, the world around you is counting on you.

You don't have to choose to be on other people's teams, but if you make the commitment to God, friends, family, an organization, a church, a team, or to anything else, you're a part of something bigger than yourself. So act like it. Give it everything you've got for the good of others.

Will you fail? Yes, you're not perfect, right? But when you fail, get back up; take responsibility for your failure, and work to get better. Why? Because your actions don't just affect you. They affect others in your life as well.

One Body, Many Parts

"All of life is a team sport." That phrase sounds like it would make a great bumper sticker or t-shirt message, doesn't it? But it's more than a catchy saying. It's a biblical truth.

"Just as each of us has one body with many members, and these members do not all have the same function, so in Christ we, though many,

form one body, and each member belongs to all the others" (Romans 12:4-5).

In this passage and several others, Paul compares the church to a body. It has many members who serve different roles. But their efforts are all unified as a part of one body. And did you catch the last phrase?

Each of us *belongs* to all the others!

Just like I belonged to the Philadelphia Eagles, the San Francisco 49ers, and for one year, the Detroit Lions.

Notice it didn't say that you just belong to the people you like or the people you're most alike.

I couldn't pull away from someone on my team because I thought they were obnoxious—or because they were hard for me to get along with. Part of the challenge of being on a team is working through hard issues with people who say or do stupid and offensive things.

Likewise, you can't separate yourself from other Christ-followers who say or do things you don't like. God is patient with all of us in our stupidity, so we have to be patient with others as well.

Starters and Role Players

When I was ready to give up my NFL dream before it even started in 1997, Erika's words of encouragement kept me going. She is my most important teammate, and from the time we started getting close, her words have carried more weight in my life than anybody's.

Her encouragement has kept me going at times like nothing else could.

My relationship with Erika reminds me of this passage in Ecclesiastes: *"Two are better than one, because they have a good return for their work: If one falls down, his friend can help him up. But pity the man who falls and has no one to help him up!" (Ecclesiastes 4:9-10).*

Erika has been my best friend and biggest supporter for nearly half my life. But I've also had others throughout my life that supported and encouraged me in ways that were critical in different seasons of life.

It started with my parents. My dad, Jon Akers, showed me a work ethic and discipline that was one of the reasons for my NFL success. And my mom, Lyn, gave me lots of encouragement through the ups and downs of my early athletic efforts. She was a committed "soccer mom" who drove me wherever I needed to go for years as I developed the leg that allowed me to pursue my dream.

Both Mom and Dad helped me with hours of kicking practice. My dad has permanent knee indentions from all the times he held the ball for me. And my mom ran for miles over the years picking up footballs and placing them in a sack for me to reload and kick again.

My brother, Rob, has also been an important part of my life. Like all siblings, we haven't always treated each other with respect. But Rob has always had my back. When we were younger, he let his little brother tag along when most big brothers wouldn't. I still smile when I think about how Rob kept me in line when we were kids by threatening to call "Officer Kowalski" whenever I caused trouble. Of course, "Officer Kowalski" didn't exist.

It continued in high school with Roy Walton and through my college and professional career with other coaches and teammates.

When I married Erika, I inherited two other incredible teammates as well: my mother-in-law and father-in-law, Sven and DeeAnn Ekman. I have friends who struggle with their in-laws, but not me. My in-laws have accepted and supported me as if I were their own.

You'd probably expect that all of these people would be a part of my life team. But one of the greatest moments of encouragement in my life came from the most unlikely source—an opposing team's coach.

In 1994, then Governor of Kentucky started an annual tradition that has lasted to this day. It's the annual football game between the University of Kentucky and Louisville University. The two schools hadn't played a football game against each other in seventy years before the governor brought the two teams back together for the Governor's Cup.

The media got behind the game and made it a big deal statewide.

It was in my sophomore year, and it was the worst pressure I had ever felt in a game, up to that time. It was my first chance to go to the University of Kentucky's Commonwealth Stadium to show the Kentucky coaching staff that they'd made a mistake by not offering me a scholarship. I would also have more friends watching than usual because it was in my hometown. I felt like all eyes were on me, and I psyched out myself.

Kentucky won the first Governor's Cup by six points, and I missed my only two kicks of the game. The two kicks that could've tied the game

It was my first real taste of public failure. My misses were covered statewide in the print and electronic media. And I began to wonder if I had what it takes to be a Division I college kicker, let alone a pro kicker.

A few days after the game, I was in a grocery store and I heard two gray-haired ladies talking about me. They had no idea I was standing right next to them.

"Did you hear that Louisville's kicker, that Akers' kid, tried to hang himself?" one asked the other.

"No, but after the game he had last weekend, it doesn't surprise me," her friend responded.

"Well, he wasn't successful," the first woman continued. "When he went to kick out the chair, he missed!"

"Oh, that's just awful!" her friend protested as she tried to hold back her laughter.

A couple of seconds later they both burst out giggling.

Are you kidding me? I thought. *Even two old ladies are slamming on me!*

Later that week, I received a hand-written letter in the mail from Bill Curry, Kentucky's head coach. He said he knew my missed kicks were painful for me, and he was writing to encourage me.

The letter said, "David, keep your head up, walk tall, and know in your heart that you'll make many more kicks in life. This is just a setback."

I couldn't believe it. The opposing team's coach actually took the time to encourage me! Coach Curry and I didn't really know each other very well. He had asked me to come to Kentucky as a walk-on, but Louisville had offered me a scholarship. There was no way I could sign on with a college—no matter how much I wanted to—without a scholarship.

Coach Curry never knew how much his letter meant to me. But it really did give me the courage to keep my head up.

"But **encourage one another daily,** *as long as it is called 'Today,' so that none of you may be hardened by sin's deceitfulness"* (Hebrews 3:13, emphasis added).

It's not only sin's deceitfulness that hardens us. It's also our failures and trials.

"Therefore encourage one another and build each other up" (1 Thessalonians 5:11).

Now fast-forward to 2013. I was watching a late-season college football game between inner-state rivals, Auburn and Alabama. I struggled with a lot of internal emotion as Auburn's kicker, Cade Foster, missed a couple of kicks early in the game that eventually cost Auburn the win. I watched him hang his head on the sidelines every time the camera focused on him.

I turned to Erika, who was sitting next to me on the couch,

and said, "Ah, man, that's painful to watch! I've totally been there! Man, this guy's in for a tough week."

"You know what?" she replied. "You should reach out to him like Bill Curry did for you when you were in the same situation. Seriously, it would probably be a huge encouragement to him."

I followed Erika's suggestion and tracked down Cade's telephone number—with the help of my agent. I found out that he was getting slammed through social media. He had even gotten some death threats. So, the next day, I called him to let him know I had been in his shoes (well, actually his cleats). I was able to say the same type of things that Coach Curry said me.

I paid forward to Cade what Coach Curry had done for me.

Like Roy Walton said a long time ago, there's no such thing as a self-made man. God brings all kinds of people into our lives that make up our life team. Some are starters who play most of the game—like Erika. And some are role players who come off the bench at key moments in our lives—like Coach Curry.

Who are the starters and role players in your life?

Pulling Away

It was the best of times, and it was the worst of times. No, I'm not suddenly quoting classical literature. (I already told you I'm not a big reader.) I'm describing my two years in San Francisco, playing for the 49ers.

I had a great year in 2011. My first field goal of the year was a fifty-nine yarder, and my season took off from there. I hit a lot of big kicks and scored a lot of points—and the team started counting on me more and more. It was a great bounce-back from that horrible 2010 finish in the playoffs.

Our team kept winning games and commentators started looking at us as real contenders for the Lombardi trophy. Coach Jim Harbaugh was a great fit for our team, and we all responded well to his leadership. Life was good.

I started to get some weird aching pains in my lower abdominal muscles late in the season, but I was able to push through into the play-offs, where I also kicked well.

I was named to the Pro Bowl for the sixth time, and I thought I was going to get that ever-elusive Super Bowl ring.

So, there we were in the NFC Championship—my sixth time to play in it. I had only won this game once, though, so I was pumped about our possibility of going to the Super Bowl.

We took the game into overtime, and once again, I was on the losing team.

Ugh, will I ever get another chance at a Super Bowl win?

After the Pro Bowl, I couldn't ignore the pain in my abs. I saw some of my old Eagles doctors. (Man, these guys are amazing! I still talk to them about issues, and they never hesitate to help me.) They diagnosed me with a "sports hernia."

Since then, my surgeon has taught me to call it "athletic pubalgia." No offense, but "sports hernia" is a lot easier to say!

I had surgery in February and I started rehabbing the next day. Rehab took longer than expected, but I felt ready by the start of the 2012 season.

We started the season against the Packers in Green Bay, where I hit my first three field goals in the first half. The first was a for-ty-three yarder, the second was a forty yarder, and the third was, well, one of the greatest moments in my career. It was a moment where all my years of practice, practice, practice paid off.

Our Offense was in hurry-up mode as the clock ticked down to half-time. We were on the Packers 45 yard line. Our quarterback, Alex Smith, threw an incomplete pass to stop the clock. It was fourth down. I looked to Coach Harbaugh and Special Teams Coach, Brad Seely, to see if they wanted to go for it.

Harbaugh paused a moment to think, and then yelled:
"Field goal! Field goal!"

I knew right away, this kick was not just an attempt for
three points. It was an attempt to tie the NFL record for longest
field goal ever.

My adrenaline was pumping, and I kept telling myself not to over-
kick the ball. Anytime I over-kicked it, I would pull or shank it. Just like
when you over-swing in golf.

Just smooth it! Just smooth it! I kept saying to myself as I lined up the
kick with Andy Lee as my Holder. I took a deep breath, like I'd done
thousands of times before, and I gave the okay to Andy.

The last thing I thought was, *Just another kick.*

And then the snap came, the hold went down, and the kick went up.
Well, actually, it went slightly up. It had to be flatter than usual to go the
distance.

As soon as the ball left my foot, I thought, *David, you idiot!
You didn't over kick it! You under kicked it!*

All the times I made this record kick in practice. And now,
when it counted, I was sure I was going to miss it.

Wait a minute, I thought, *This may be closer than I expected.
Maybe a foot short.... No, it's going to hit the cross bar.... Oh, it did hit
the cross bar!*

The ball bounced up, and from sixty-three yards away, I couldn't tell
if it bounced back or through the uprights. I quickly looked at the refs
standing underneath the goal post.

C'mon! Give it to me! Give it to me!

The ref's hands went straight up.

They gave it to me! It's GOOOOOOOOOOOOOOD!

The field goal team came running to me and hoisted me up on their
shoulders. They knew *I* hadn't just kicked the record-tying field goal.

They had as well.

That's how it works with a team.

It looked like I should just set up residency in Hawaii. I was surely going to another Pro Bowl that year. Unfortunately, that would be my last great personal moment as a Niner.

About a month later, on a cold, rainy day, I fell while practicing field goals. Our practice field was made of a new kind of turf that didn't have much grip, and the rain only made the turf slicker.

When I say I fell, I'm talking about a Charlie Brown fall where my legs went straight up and I landed on my head.

I finished my drills and went home. When I returned to practice the next day and began kicking, I could feel the same sensation that I felt when I first got the sports hernia a year earlier. And like the first time, it got progressively worse.

I started losing power, and I couldn't drive my leg all the way through the kick. The injury started to affect me on a day-to-day basis. And then it started to affect my game performance in a mid-season battle against the New Orleans Saints. That's when I first missed a field goal attempt and had another one blocked.

That night, I flew with the team back to San Francisco, and the next day, my training staff put me on a redeye to Philadelphia to meet with the surgeon who'd performed the sports-hernia surgery. He found a lot of inflammation in the same area and gave me eight injections of cortisone in my lower abdominal area. It was some of the worst pain I had ever felt! I flew back to San Francisco the next day, and although I felt better, I still didn't feel good.

We flew to St. Louis later that week for a conference game against the Rams. I made three field goals during the game, and it went to overtime. But it was the one I didn't hit that caused a media storm.

I missed a fifty-one yarder by three inches on the right upright, and we lost the game.

The social media comments began to flood in about my missed field goals. To top it off, the house we were renting flooded. The old saying, "When it rains, it pours," never seemed truer.

I started to get down on myself, but I was resolved to push through the pain and keep kicking for my team. Despite the criticism, I still felt the support of the 49ers organization—until the last game of the season against the Arizona Cardinals, when I missed two more kicks, and the 49ers quickly signed another kicker. Although I was still a part of the team, I knew my days with San Francisco were numbered.

We all knew that I needed to get off my leg and let it heal. The more I kicked, the worse it got. And if the social media response was bad before, now it was a nightmare.

Spiritually, I was trying to draw close to God for His strength to get through it. But I was definitely questioning what was happening.

I also was pulling away from people.

I wouldn't respond to anyone who tried to encourage me. I felt like I was on the outs with the team, and my emotional struggle turned into depression.

Physical pain is one thing, but public humiliation is another. I'm letting everyone down. My coaches. My teammates. The fans. Even my family.

I continued to push my friends away, and my marriage was the closest it had ever been to dissolving. I was a wreck, and I was taking it out on the ones I loved the most—Erika and the kids. It was hard on Erika because she knew I was really struggling, but the more she tried to pull me out of my funk, the more angry and disconnected I was.

We got a first-round bye in the playoffs, and then we beat the Green Bay Packers to play the Atlanta Falcons in the NFC championship game. I missed a thirty-eight yard field goal attempt that could've cost us the game. I clanged it off the top eyelet of the upright, and it bounced straight up in the air. No good.

Fortunately, we won the game, but my miss only furthered media speculation about my place with the 49ers. Some were wondering if I would hurt the team by missing a field goal in the Super Bowl.

The champagne was flowing in the locker room after we beat the Falcons, but I wasn't enjoying it. Reporters were asking me if I thought the 49ers were going to fire me.

The upside is that we were headed to New Orleans where we'd play the Baltimore Ravens in the Super Bowl. I was once again back at the pinnacle of football success. But unlike the first time, I wasn't enjoying any of it. I didn't want any family or friends to come to be a part of it with me. I just wanted to be alone.

The two week lead-up to the Super Bowl was brutal as fan social media and network- and cable-sports media came down hard on me for my recent misses. I had to stop listening to it.

I had some great teammates, who encouraged and supported me all through my struggles that season, but I pulled away from them, too, because I felt like I'd let them down. Vernon Davis, Frank Gore, Brian Jennings, Andy Lee, Justin Smith, and Patrick Willis were some of the best teammates I could ask for. They always supported me publically and encouraged me privately.

But I kept pulling away.

Once we got to New Orleans, I didn't want to leave my hotel room. When I did, someone would yell out a comment like, "I hope you don't blow this game, too!"

Fortunately, on Super Bowl day, I was able to rise to the occasion and hit all three of my field goals. We fell behind early and fought our way back in the second half—after the lights went out in the stadium and stopped the game for thirty-four minutes. I felt good that I helped give the team a chance to win the game in the final seconds. But we came up short when we reached the five yard line and couldn't

get the ball over the goal line in three attempts.
This was the last time I would dress in a Niners jersey, and the emotions overwhelmed me after the game as I sat in the locker room of the Super Dome.

The 2012 season is when I kicked the longest field goal of my career—which tied for the longest field goal in NFL history. And it's the season when I returned to my second Super Bowl. And, yet, I was in a life struggle that took the joy out of all of it.

The final hardship of the season came about a month after the Super Bowl when the 49ers made it official what I expected was coming. They released me and didn't fulfill the final year of my contract.

I couldn't really blame them. My leg was not what it was the year before. It was no longer a leg that could be trusted in big games.

After the season, my emotional spiral continued, and I began to pull away from God, too. It continued to get worse until I happened to pick up a book called *Ninety Minutes in Heaven*, by Don Piper. To this day, I don't know where I got the book. I know I didn't buy it, and I never figured out who had given it to me.

It was like the book just appeared. And it was exactly what I needed to read.

The book really connected with me at both a head-level and a heart-level. And God used it to inspire change in my life. I realized Don and I had some things in common. We both internalized our problems and didn't allow people into our lives that wanted to reach out to us. We didn't let God's people use their gifts to build us up.

I realized that even though I'm part of the body of Christ, I had cut myself off from the body I so desperately needed.

Ninety Minutes in Heaven showed me how much I need the people God has placed in my life. And when I don't open up and share my struggles with my life team, I'm setting myself up to fall even harder.

I eventually came around and started restoring my relationship with God and my life team again. And once I did, God began to restore my joy and peace. The depression went away, and Erika got her husband back—and my kids got their dad back.

I learned through my rough patch in 2012 that hard times could make it hard to connect with people. But that's exactly when we need people the most.

You need a team of people around you. I have a message for you if, in your struggle, you've pulled away from others who love you. You can't make it on your own.

You're not a self-made man or woman, so stop trying to go it alone.

Extra Point:

I am very aware that the body of Christ needs even the parts that seem strange or unique. Why? Because my role in football sometimes seemed unique—or even strange—to teammates and fans. Even though the name of the game is football, some people think that the kicking game is an add-on to the real game of scoring touchdowns.

I know my talent may seem unique. At no other time in history, up until the last half century, could a guy make a great salary kicking an oblong leather ball through two posts.

But kickers are a critical part of the NFL game. In fact, most of the top scorers in NFL history are kickers. At the time of this writing, I'm eleventh on the all-time scoring list myself.

Kickers score a lot of the team's points.

But I know that being a kicker makes me different from other players on my team. My teammates have always joked with me that I have the easiest job during the practice week. I don't have to hit, block, tackle, or be tackled. But they also tell me that they wouldn't want my job on Sunday, when I'm expected to make every kick in front of millions of people.

Let me put it another way: Everyone on the team wants my job during the practice week, but no one wants my job on game day.

Even the best quarterbacks are expected to miss forty percent of their passes. Incomplete passes often go unnoticed, because one incomplete pass doesn't usually kill a drive or stop points from going on the board.

It was different with me. Most of the time, if I was on the field, I was trying to score points. My success, or failure, was black and white. I would either hit the kick, score points, and come through for my team, or I would miss the kick, not put points on the board, and let my team down.

If I hit my kicks, I was just doing my job. If I missed my kicks, I cost our team points—or worse, a loss. I wasn't doing my job.

For a good part of the game, I sat on the sidelines, irrelevant to the outcome. But when the game was on the line, the weight of the win often rested on my shoulders...or rather, my leg.

So, yeah, I'm definitely one of the unique parts of my team. And that has given me a heart for those who feel like they don't fit in the body of Christ. Those who think they're too strange or unique.

But I'm here to tell you that the body of Christ needs you.

"The eye cannot say to the hand, 'I don't need you!' And the head cannot say to the feet, 'I don't need you!' On the contrary, those parts of the body that seem to be weaker are indispensible" (1 Corinthians 12: 21-22).

No matter how different you are, you belong on this team.

Kicking off during my University of Louisville days [1994]

CHAPTER NINE

Shine Your Light

[Platform]

---

*"It's about the journey—mine and yours—
and the lives we can touch, the legacy
we can leave, and the world we can
change for the better."*

– TONY DUNGY –

And you have an important role to play.

Don't let anyone else convince you otherwise.

During the course of my NFL career, I lived in three different areas of the U.S. And every place I lived, I believed God put me there for a reason. Not just to play football, but also to be a part of the work He was doing in that community.

Being a part of an NFL team gave me a very public presence in each local area. It gave me a platform from which to work. And I always tried to use that God-given platform—along with my God-given salary—to bless other people.

In chapter three, I shared about the work I did with Children's Hospital of Philadelphia through my foundation, Kicks for Kids. In Chapter four, I shared about the families I gave to in Medford, New Jersey. These were just a few things I had the privilege of being a part of during my time with the Eagles.

In chapters five and eight, I told you about Christian Huang and San Francisco City Impact (SFCI), the ministry I participated in while we lived in San Francisco. The purpose of the organization was to reach out to the poor and suffering in San Francisco and help them discover a whole new life in Jesus.

After hearing Christian talk about the street ministry that SFCI was doing, I knew I had to be a part of it.

My first experience working with SFCI was in the Tenderloin District of San Francisco, a poor and densely populated area known for its blatant sin. Basically, this is San Fran's version of Skid Row. It's a place full of pimps, prostitutes, drug dealers, drug users, alcoholics, and lost and broken people of all kinds. It's a dirty, smelly, sad, and evil part of the city. Most would say it's a place where the forgotten and unloved hang out.

But because of SFCI, the people there are neither forgotten, nor unloved.

I went with Christian and our friend, Nate Hansen, to take

part in SFCI's "Adopt a Building" ministry outreach. Our plan for
the day was to visit people where they live, in their apartment
buildings. I was so pumped up to be a part of this ministry! I was ready
to be a light in a dark place.

Our activity that day would take place in Boyd's Hotel—
an old, abandoned, seven-story apartment building that had
once been a hotel.

As we walked into the building, Christian asked me,
"Do you think anyone will recognize you?"

"Nah, I highly doubt it," I replied. "If we were in Philly there might
be a chance, but not here. Besides, who would ever think
that an NFL player would be down at the Boyd?"

We went from one dingy and dilapidated apartment room
to the next, checking in on people to see how we could help them. Offering to pray for them.

As we passed by one of the rooms, I felt the presence of
evil draping over me. It was so thick that I struggled to breathe.
I glanced in the room and spotted the image of skulls and other death
symbols—not to mention some weird, almost ghostly lighting.

I quickly turned to Christian and asked, "Bro, who lives in there?
This place gives me the creeps!"

"That's because this is where the building drug dealer lives. When
people in the neighborhood get their checks at the beginning of each
month, this guy passes out drugs like it's candy."

"Wow! No wonder this place is putting off such a creepy vibe!"
I responded as a shiver ran down my spine.

We moved on to other rooms, and man, I can't even describe
how deplorable the living conditions were. The building's residents
didn't have much, and what they did have was worn, dirty, smelly,
and grimy.

It was all fairly hard to stomach. But I had no idea

what lay ahead.

David's Room

We eventually walked into the most deplorable room
imaginable. The man who lived there was named David. The first thing
that greeted us, even before we walked through the doorway, was a foul,
horrific odor. I can't describe the smell. It was a blend of human feces,
body odor, mildew, garbage, urine, and a few other things I couldn't
identify. It was a smell that has stayed with me ever since. I nearly threw
up before I even stepped into the room.

It only got worse inside the room. The floor was covered
with trash, soiled clothing, and—are you ready for this? David's crap. Yes,
you read that correctly, and I'm not speaking metaphorically.
It was literally human crap.

I could be a little more careful and call it *feces*, but when it's on the
floor all around you, *feces* is too delicate of a term. Too civilized.

As I was dodging all the "land mines" on the floor, I managed
to look up and see an elderly-looking man lying in a bed in the
middle of the room. He was in the fetal position on a sheet-less bed, with
tattered jeans, no socks, and no shirt.

As I stepped closer, I could see him more clearly—and I
realized he was probably much younger than he looked. His gray hair
hadn't been washed in weeks. It was long, straggly, and matted. If it had
been combed, it probably would've looked a little like the unstyled, long
hair that hippies would've worn in that area
fifty years earlier.

David was noticeably in pain. His breathing was quick and
labored—and he wheezed and moaned every time he inhaled. He had
a large breathing tube that came out of his nose and into a breathing
machine that sat on the floor next to his bed.

His skin was pale and pasty, and it drooped from his body. He had
EKG stickers stuck in random places, left over from his last trip to the

emergency room.

David didn't seem to mind us too much, but he didn't respond to us much either—at least, not at first. He just concentrated on his breathing.

I felt so badly for him, and my mind raced in all different directions.

How did he get here?

Where is his family?

I'm sure he's had a pretty hard life. Should I ask him why he's in such bad shape? Is that too personal?

I just want him to know I care. How do I tell him that without coming off like an insensitive jerk?

Maybe we should show him we care before we try to tell him.

As I was asking myself these questions, my eyes darted all around the room.

There were soiled clothes, hospital gowns, and EKG stickers all over the floor. It was clear that David had no control over his bodily functions and no family or friends who cared enough to help him.

Along one wall, there was an old chest of drawers that was stocked with food—all of it rotten. Oh, and there was one unopened bottle of Gatorade.

Really? Gatorade? Is this because he wants to make sure he's properly hydrated?

Nothing in his room made sense. David didn't have a refrigerator or oven. Heck, he didn't even have a sink.

We began to ask him questions to see what his needs were.

"How are you doing, Dave," I asked.

"How do you think I'm doing!" he shot back in a crackly voice.

Wow! This guy is really angry.

Over the course of the next twenty minutes or so, we found out that David had once been a pastor while living in Iowa, but he had since faced some pretty tough circumstances and had given up on God. He told us he was very sick—both physically and emotionally. And that he was pretty much confined to his room.

We talked to him about Jesus, and he told us that he had reaffirmed his faith. But he was deeply hurting. He didn't have much to live for.

As we sized up his physical needs, it was clear that David needed fresh food and clean clothing. But more than anything, he needed his room cleaned up. So, we went to City Impact's food bank and shelter to get some food, clothing, and cleaning supplies. And when we got back to his room, we began scrubbing away. We cleaned up all the trash (that was the easy part) and then had to do something about the piles of crap that were scattered all over the floor.

At that point, I began to get a sense that we were doing what Jesus would be doing for David if He were still here on earth. Then I thought about how Jesus is still here on earth—ministering through His followers, through those of us who were standing in David's room.

We were the hands and feet of Christ in that moment— showing David God's extreme love for him.

I'm not going to sanitize it for you, though. I started to get the floor wet so I could mop up the EKG stickers, crusted food, and dried feces. And I was shocked—although I don't know why— by the development of what I can only describe as "doo-doo stew."

Oh my, it was disgusting. I had to go into "daddy-diaper-changing" mode—stat! (Fortunately, years of changing my kids' dirty diapers had prepared me a little for this!)

My nostrils began to close up, which was actually a good

thing! Nate and I trudged on—mopping, scrubbing, scraping, and yes, gagging.

Christian is normally able to attack these situations as aggressively and tenaciously as a boxer going in for a knockout, but this time, he was the one who got knocked out. He ran out of the room, dry heaving, and Nate and I burst out laughing.

I turned to Nate and did my best Jase Robertson (from Duck Dynasty) impersonation: "He gone!"

We continued to clean and scrub until there was nothing left on the floor. The wretched smell that was there before was replaced by the scent of antibacterial disinfectants.

We stepped back and marveled at the room's transformation. It was like Extreme Makeover—the Skid Row Edition.

After basking in our sense of accomplishment for a few minutes, we approached David's bed and began talking to him again about his relationship with Jesus.

"I know Jesus," he responded.

"You really do?" I questioned with a little too much surprise.

"Yeah, but I'm starting to wonder if you guys do," he halfheartedly joked.

We all laughed. It was good to see him crack a smile.

"Can we pray for you?" I continued.

He nodded.

"How can we pray?"

He said he had been in a lot of pain lately, and he was ready to go to heaven. He asked us to pray that he would die and go to be with Jesus.

"You really want to die?" I probed.

"Yes! I really want to die!" he affirmed in no uncertain terms.

He really wanted to be in a place where there was no more pain.

Now.

He really wanted to be with God.

Now.

Okay, time out. This was not what I expected street ministry to be like. I thought it would be an opportunity to pray with people to accept Christ. But David had already done that. And I expected it to be a chance to pray for people to be healed. But that's not what David wanted.

I *wasn't* expecting to pray that someone would die!

But that's how deplorable the conditions are in so many people's lives. They'd rather be dead than alive. But most of us aren't willing to go and wade into the crap of people's lives—figuratively and literally—to help make their lives any better.

So, what did I do? I did what David asked me to do. There was no "Kumbaya" moment that day. Instead, I prayed that David would die so he would be able to experience ultimate healing in heaven with his Father. I pleaded with all my heart that the Lord would take David home to be with Him.

A few weeks later, David was out and about in the Tenderloin district. Christian and his wife, Cori, saw David and stopped to take a picture with him. He looked so much better! God gave him a few months of relief from his suffering. And not too long later, God welcomed David into Heaven.

David is no longer suffering.

We All Have a Platform

Every one of us has a platform from which we can serve others. We each have a sphere of influence where we can have a profound impact on people's lives. One of the key components of *winning in life* is using your platform to serve and bless others.

We all have a different platform. As an NFL player, the size of my platform has been big at times. And I've always felt a sense of responsibility to use that platform for God's glory.

That's why every time I made a field goal, I would look up to heaven and point to God. It became my trademark, just like Tim Tebow's kneel to pray in the end zone became his. It was my way of acknowledging that the skill to kick field goals, and the opportunity to play in the NFL, were given to me by God. It was my way of saying "thank you" in a very public way.

It was one of the ways I used my public platform.

I also took opportunities in media interviews to talk about my passion for Jesus, and I used my NFL platform to put on outreach concerts that featured artists like TobyMac, Jeremy Camp, and Brandon Heath.

But like everyone, I had a less-public, everyday platform, as well. With my family. With my co-workers (my teammates and coaches). In my church. In my neighborhood. And in my community.

I tried to make the most of that platform just as much as I tried to make the most of my NFL platform.

Jesus talked a lot about letting our light shine to other people from the platform of our lives.

"You are the light of the world. A town on a hill cannot be hidden. Neither do people light a lamp and put it under a bowl. Instead they put it on its stand, and it gives light to everyone in the house" (Matthew 5:14-15).

Jesus wants our light to be visible to others. So, why would I try to hide it? I've always wanted people to see my light.

"Let your light shine before others, that they may see your good deeds and glorify your Father in heaven" (Matthew 5:16).

How do you let your light shine? Through actions. Through good deeds.

So, whether I was on a very public platform as an NFL player or a smaller platform as an ordinary guy doing ordinary life stuff, I've tried to shine my light by doing good things for people in Jesus' name.

What is your platform? Think about it for a moment. Who are the people that you influence? What good deeds are you doing to shine your light?

Along the Way

There are two kinds of ministry that I've seen at work: "Out of the way" and "Along the way."

"Out of the way" ministry is what Christian, Nate, and I did when we went into a different neighborhood than our own to reach out to *"the least of these"* that Jesus talked about in Matthew 25. Instead of making them come to us—which they wouldn't— we went to them.

"Along the way" ministry is when God puts people in your path who have a need in that moment—and you're willing to slow down, recognize their need, and engage with them about it. It requires you to have your radar up so you can be sensitive to the people around you as you interact with them in the normal course of your day.

And it requires you to be sensitive to the leading of God's Spirit so you can "feel" His nudge when He wants you to minister to someone—along the way of your everyday life.

Maybe it's your co-worker, who's going through a hard time at home. Maybe it's the waitress who's a little grouchy because something's wrong. Maybe it's your neighbor who hasn't cut his grass or fixed a broken fence in a while. Or maybe it's the kid down the street who doesn't have a father figure in his life.

Or maybe it's the beggar you pass on the street.

I'm not always as sensitive as I want to be to the needs of other people. Even as I write this, I'm convicted that I need—and want—

to do more. But here's an example of an "along the way" ministry moment from my life. A time when I think I got it right.
A time when I was sensitive and responded to God's leading.

Around the same time that I did the "Adopt a Building"
outreach with SFCI, I had to travel to Minneapolis for a game against the Minnesota Vikings. I was walking from the hotel to a restaurant where I was going to meet my family for dinner when
I came across a sloppily dressed man who was asking for money.

Now, I had just learned from Christian and Francis Chan that
I shouldn't give money to people I don't know. I had been fairly consistent about giving street beggars money when I came across them in the past. I always felt like it wasn't up to me to be
responsible for what they were going to do with the money.

I was always asking the question in my mind: *Are they hungry, or do they just want to buy some booze with this money?*

I would give them the benefit of the doubt, and just give them some money—and then walk away.

But Francis and Christian taught me a different way.
Instead of just giving them money, they challenged me to start
a conversation and get to know the person whose hand was out. Rather than just placating my conscience, it was a way of
recognizing their value as a human-being made in God's image. When you start seeing street beggars as people that God created
and loves, you stop seeing them as "street trash." (I'm sorry to put it so bluntly, but isn't it easy to discard people on the street like we would a piece of trash? I'm just sayin'... .)

Many people that you meet on the street know about Jesus. But they've never really seen or experienced Him. When we engage with them on a relational level, we have the chance to show Jesus to them. We can make Him real for those who aren't ready to talk about Him.

So, when I came across this man on the street in Minneapolis,
I stopped and looked him in the eye.

He had a hard time looking back at me. "I need five bucks. You got five bucks?" he muttered.

"Are you hungry?" I asked.

"I just need five bucks," he repeated.

"Look, bro, if you're hungry, I'll go get you some food. But if you only want money, it ain't happening."

He nodded and said, "Yeah, I'm hungry."

I told him to come with me, and we searched together for a restaurant where I could buy him something to eat. We found a nice place, and we sat at a table together.

I told him, "You order whatever you want."

He ordered a rack of barbecued ribs and some chicken wings.

"Anything else sound good?" I offered.

"No, this is great," he replied and then paused. "Oh, and could I have a Coke, too…please?"

I had already shown him I cared about his physical needs, and now I had the chance to engage with him at a relational level. He shared that he'd jumped a train from Jacksonville, Florida, because he needed to get out of town. He didn't tell me exactly why he needed to get away, but he did open up about his drug and alcohol addictions. He confessed that he would've taken the five bucks he was begging for to buy some booze.

I said, "Bro, I knew that. I wanted to help you, not hurt you by supporting your addictions."

I paused, and he didn't respond, so I continued.

"I also want you to know that Jesus loves you."

He wrinkled up his face. "I'm not sure what you mean."

"The reason I'm doing this is because I'm living my life according to what Jesus taught in the Bible. And He tells us to love Him and other people. And then He says the way to show my love for others is to feed them when they're hungry. I love you, man, and I don't want you to be hungry."

He nodded and thanked me.

"There's one more thing I want to share with you," I added. "We all have a spiritual hunger that's a lot like our physical hunger. And I've learned that there's only one thing that can fill that spiritual hunger—the love of Jesus. He loves you and wants you to draw close to Him. He can give you a different kind of life if you seek after Him. He will provide for your needs like He did today when He led me to cross your path. Give Him a chance to change your life."

We talked a while longer, and then I moved on to meet my family. I doubt that I'll ever know this side of heaven if my words made a difference in his life. But I did what Jesus called me to do. I loved this stranger with my actions and words. I demonstrated His worth by doing more than handing him five bucks and walking away. And I planted the seeds I knew I was supposed to plant.

"So neither he who plants nor he who waters is anything, but only God who makes things grow" (1 Corinthians 3:7).

Maybe I planted the seeds. Maybe I watered them. But the rest is in God's hands. Only He can change a life.

"It was great to win the Super Bowl, but really and truly what you're going to leave on this Earth is your influence on others."

- JOE GIBBS -

Another "Along the Way" Moment

Here's another "along the way" moment that I missed. Fortunately, Erika didn't miss it.

We were on our way to a concert on a double-date night with another couple from the Bay area. We went out to grab a cup of coffee before the show at my favorite coffee shop, Blue Bottle.

I was really pumped. I was getting my favorite latte with my favorite person in the world, and the whole night was ahead of us.

As I walked up to the counter to order, I noticed a disheveled man who had also walked up to the counter just a ways down from me. I didn't pay too much attention to him, but Erika did. She began a conversation with the man and found out he was extremely hungry.

Since the coffee shop didn't have much food, Erika left the store with the man and found a deli just around the corner, where she could get him some food.

I'm thinking, *We don't have our order yet! Where is she going!?*

Our friends told me Erika had found out about the deli and was taking the man there. So we all shot out of the coffee shop to catch up with them. When we arrived at the deli, Erika and the man were already on their way out, and the man had two large plastic bags in his hands—full of food.

"If anyone has material possessions and sees his brother or sister in need but has no pity on him, how can the love of God be in that person? Dear children, let us not love with words or speech but with actions and in truth" (1 John 3:17-18).

We talk a lot about love, but how many of us really take the time and make the effort to love with our actions? Like Jesus did?

You may think that we didn't really accomplish anything in the two "along-the-way" stories I just shared. I'll be honest, I've thought that myself. But I can't worry about what we accomplished. Our job is to be obedient. God's job is to accomplish something through it.

What would happen if every Christ-follower responded to the needs of people all around them—at work, in their neighborhoods, and as they go to restaurants, the bank, or Wal-Mart?

How would that change people's view of Christianity?
How would it change the world?

I can't change what everyone else does—and neither can you. But
we can change what we do. We can make sure that we're acting as Jesus'
hands and feet to those who have great need.

I believe that one of the most important ways that we can *win in
spite of* the problems in our life is to stop thinking about our own needs
and think about the needs of others.

And then do something about the other person's needs.

When you get your eyes off yourself and focus on others, your
problems seem less pressing and painful. Your perspective changes, and
you begin to see all that you have when you see what "the least of these"
don't have.

You become more thankful. You become more compassionate. You
become more merciful.

You become the hands and feet of Jesus.

I constantly think of Jesus' own words in Matthew 25:40:
*"I tell you, whatever you did for the least of these brothers and
sisters of mine, you did for me."*

Jesus says that when we feed those who are hungry, we
feed Him. When we give the thirsty something to drink, we give
Him something to drink. When we invite in a stranger, we invite
Him in. When we give clothes to those who don't have enough,
we give clothes to Him. And when we visit prisoners—those who
have messed up their lives and other people's lives—we visit
Jesus *(Matthew 25:35-36).*

Now, I don't know how it works that when I fed the man
in Minneapolis, I was feeding Jesus. I'm not smart enough to
figure it out.

But I *do know* that I have to be obedient.

So do you. Do you want to hear God say to you, "Well done!"? Then use whatever platform and whatever resources God has given you to love people—especially the *"least of these."*

If you do, you're loving Jesus.

That's true winning.

Extra Point:

What do you think of when you hear someone talk about the "mission field"? Do you think of someone with a seminary degree going to a third world country to tell the "natives" about Jesus?

Well, that may be one kind of mission field, but it's not the only kind. You have a mission field right now, exactly where you're at. And you don't have to have a seminary degree to be a missionary in your mission field. You just have to use the platform God has given you—whatever it is—to look around and serve whatever needs you find.

The "natives" you're serving are the people you can reach from your natural platform. They all need God and His grace in their lives. And they need you to usher God's love to them.

Ministry is not complicated. First, love the person who's in front of you—along the way of your life. The waitress you have at lunch, the co-worker who works close to you at work, and the homeless guy you pass on the street all need God's love through you.

And then ask God if He wants to send you to a place of great need somewhere else in your community or in other parts of the world. When I've asked, He's given me new friends and ministry partners who have influenced me to go into all kinds of places I wouldn't have otherwise gone. Like the Tenderloin District of San Francisco.

People have needs everywhere. So, God is looking for hands, feet, and mouths who are willing to minister wherever He leads. He leads some to minister to the poor in places like the Tenderloin District, and He leads others to minister to the wealthy—who often live in spiritual poverty.

He leads some to leave everything familiar and go to far-away places, and He leads some to minister locally.

"But you will receive power when the Holy Spirit comes upon you; and you will be my witnesses in Jerusalem, and all Judea and Samaria, and to the ends of the earth" (Acts 1:8).

Here's my personal interpretation of this verse: "But you will receive power when the Holy Spirit comes upon you; and you will be my witnesses in Nashville, all Tennessee the U.S., and to the ends of the earth" (Acts 1:8, David Akers' Edition).

How would this verse read for you?

Wherever you go, God has promised to go with you. After calling His disciples to go into the world, He said: "And surely I am with you always, to the very end..." (Matthew 28:20).

It's time to go.

Doing street ministry in the Tenderloin District of San Fransisco with City Impact [2012]

A local drug dealer's room [2012]

*Serving with **Adopt a Building Program** [2012]*

OVERTIME
It's Your Turn

Throughout this book, I've shared with you my story. Now it's your turn. Regardless of what your story has been to this point, you can change it from here on out. With God's help, you really can be a winner in spite of whatever comes your way.

It takes a lot of courage to make changes in your life. But if God has spoken to you as you've read my story, I encourage you to do whatever He's asking you to do. Remember, there's a prize waiting for those who choose to live their lives for the one-and-only cause that really counts.

Life is short. So, play to win.

Life Is Short. Play to Win.

Erika picked up the phone early on the morning of Sunday, September 21, 2014. She was surprised to hear the voice of my agent, Jerrold Colton, on the other end of the line.

"Go hug your husband, he is going to wake up to terrible news," were the first words Jerrold said. "Go hold him tight."

"I don't understand," she responded. "Do you know something I don't?"

"Yeah, I just got word that Rob Bironas was killed in a car accident last night. He lost control of his truck and ran off the road into some trees. I know David and Rob were pretty close."

Jerrold was right. As I shared earlier in this book, Rob and I had been practicing together throughout the spring and summer of 2014, thinking we might get a call from an NFL team in need of a kicker. He had a very successful career as a Kicker with the Tennessee Titans.

Because of my chronic injuries from 2012-13, I didn't get an offer for 2014. I was thinking about retiring, but to be honest, I had trained in the off-season since high school. It's all I knew. So, there I was again—training in the off-season. This time with Rob.

He and I kicked together at a local high school stadium in the Nashville area. It had a better artificial turf field than most colleges.

When my family and I first moved to Nashville, after the 2013 season, Rob had been one of the first guys to reach out and welcome us to the area. He'd been living there since his first season with the Titans.

I really enjoyed reconnecting with Rob. He was very helpful with our transition to the Nashville area. He was a warm, friendly guy, who, like me, had a young family and was considering life after the NFL.

He was just thirty-six years old when he died. Sadly, he left behind his wife, Rachel, and his son, London, who, as I previously mentioned, used to shag balls, along with my son, Luke.

Rob's premature death really impacted me. After working through the raw emotions of losing a friend, it was a reminder that life is short. For Rob, it was shorter than most. But truth is life is short whether you live to be thirty-six or ninety-six. On the other hand, eternity is long. It's infinite. It goes on forever.

Of course, that's not just a reality for me. It's a reality for you as well.

"'All men are like grass, and all their glory is like the flowers of the field; the grass withers and the flowers fall, but the word of the LORD stands forever'" (1 Peter 1:24-25).

Throughout this book, I've shared with you my firm belief in God, and how His Word has shaped everything in my life. And one of the things that the Bible teaches is that at the end of this life, there's an eternal reality of Heaven and Hell.

The Bible says that this world isn't our true home. God has designed us to be with Him in Heaven. That's why we often long for a different place—especially when we face one trial after another. We long for a place where there's no more suffering or pain.

"But our citizenship is in heaven. And we eagerly await a Savior from there, the Lord Jesus Christ, who, by the power that enables him to bring everything under his control, will transform our lowly bodies so that they will be like his glorious one" (Philippians 3:20-21).

Whether you realize it or not, the longing you get at times for something more is really a longing for Heaven. It's a longing for God.

If you're wise, you'll use the few days you have on earth to prepare for heaven, and to make an eternal difference in people's lives.

"Be very careful, then, how you live—not as unwise, but as wise, making the most of every opportunity, because the days are evil" (Ephesians 5:15-16).

I challenge you to examine your life and honestly assess what you've been living for. Are you living for your current reality in this life or your future reality in Heaven?

In Chapter three, I talked about how your perspective can change how your circumstances affect you. Well, the ultimate change in your perspective is when you view things in light of your eternal destiny, rather than your current reality in a world that can sometimes be really messed up.

It's a whole lot easier going through your current pain when you know there's a time coming when there will be no more sorrow or affliction. It helps when you know your pain is actually purifying and preparing you for Heaven.

"Therefore we do not lose heart. Though outwardly we are wasting away, yet inwardly we are being renewed day by day. For our light and momentary troubles are achieving for us an eternal glory that far outweighs them all. So we fix our eyes not on what is seen, but on what is unseen, since what is seen is temporary, but what is unseen is eternal" (2 Corinthians 4:16-18).

The Good and the Bad

In his "Pre Game Speech" at the beginning of this book, John Harbaugh made this profound statement: "You can endure a lifetime of pain for an eternity of glory."

You really can.

Of course, it's not all bad in this life. Not at all! There are moments of incredible joy, excitement, and fulfillment. I can vividly remember those amazing moments when Erika and I have felt the blessings of our relationship. And I can remember the other family moments when our children were born, or when I marveled at their growth and accomplishments. I can remember so well some of the great places I've gotten to travel, some of the great people I've gotten to meet, and some of the great games in which I've played.

And I've made it a habit to thank God for those moments

that give me a very small glimpse of what life is going to be like in Heaven.

And even though it's one of the hardest things to do, I thank God for the adversity I've had to endure—because it's made me more like Him. Yeah, you heard me right; I thank God for the pain.

Sounds crazy, right? I mean, really, who thanks God for suffering? It's not easy for me. I mean I'm not a masochist! But looking at my past trials from my current perspective, I can now see how God has made me a much-improved father, husband, teammate, friend, influencer and follower as a result of my trials.

I've been in retirement from the NFL for just a short time, and I find myself reflecting a lot on the good times and bad that happened during my time in the NFL.

And I'm left with one undeniable conclusion. When we have God's strength and wisdom at work within us, we can *win in spite of* whatever trials we face.

The key is to use the tools he's given us: Perseverance, Perspective, Priorities, Passion, Personnel, Preparation, Participation, and our Platform.

Each one plays a critical role in helping us emerge from this life as winners who get the ultimate prize: Heaven.

I look forward to the day when I get to hear God say to me: "Well done! Now your real life begins!" And I want to do everything I can in this life to assure that happens for me and as many others as possible.

Including you.

One day your game of life will be over (I don't mean the board game!) and you will either be a clear winner or a clear loser.

I challenge you again with the words of the apostle Paul that I quoted earlier in this book. And I encourage you to make this the aspiration of your life as well. I have.

"I press on to take hold of that for which Christ Jesus took hold of me. Brothers and sisters, I do not consider myself yet to have taken hold of it. But one thing I do: Forgetting what is behind and straining toward what is ahead, I press on toward the goal to win the prize for which God has called me heavenward in Christ Jesus" (Philippians 3:12-14).

The prize that's waiting for you is not a ring, or trophy, or money, or the accolades of people. The real prize for those who win in this life is getting to spend eternity with God in Heaven.

So, regardless of what your past looks like, press on to take hold of the prize.

And never give up.

Contact Information

To order additional copies of this book, please visit
www.redemption-press.com

Also available on Amazon.com and BarnesandNoble.com
Or by calling toll free 1-844-2REDEEM.

CPSIA information can be obtained
at www.ICGtesting.com
Printed in the USA
FFHW010655200519
52572066-58026FF